HBR's 10 Must Reads

UPDATED &
EXPANDED

I0112717

Innovation

HBR's 10 Must Reads

HBR's 10 Must Reads are definitive collections of classic ideas, practical advice, and essential thinking from the pages of *Harvard Business Review*. Exploring topics like disruptive innovation, emotional intelligence, and new technology in our ever-evolving world, these books empower any leader to make bold decisions and inspire others.

TITLES INCLUDE:

HBR's 10 Must Reads for New Managers
HBR's 10 Must Reads on Artificial Intelligence
HBR's 10 Must Reads on Building a Great Culture
HBR's 10 Must Reads on Change Management
HBR's 10 Must Reads on Communication
HBR's 10 Must Reads on Data Strategy
HBR's 10 Must Reads on Decision-Making
HBR's 10 Must Reads on Emotional Intelligence
HBR's 10 Must Reads on High Performance
HBR's 10 Must Reads on Innovation
HBR's 10 Must Reads on Leadership
HBR's 10 Must Reads on Leading Digital Transformation
HBR's 10 Must Reads on Leading Winning Teams
HBR's 10 Must Reads on Managing People
HBR's 10 Must Reads on Managing Yourself
HBR's 10 Must Reads on Marketing
HBR's 10 Must Reads on Mental Toughness
HBR's 10 Must Reads on Strategy
HBR's 10 Must Reads on Women and Leadership
HBR's 10 Must Reads Boxed Set (6 books)
HBR's 10 Must Reads Ultimate Boxed Set (14 books)

For a full list, visit hbr.org/mustreads.

HBR's 10 Must Reads

UPDATED &
EXPANDED

Innovation

Harvard Business Review Press
Boston, Massachusetts

HBR Press Quantity Sales Discounts

Harvard Business Review Press titles are available at significant quantity
discounts when purchased in bulk for leadership development programs, client
gifts, or sales promotions. Opportunities to co-brand copies with your logo or
messaging are also available. For details and discount information for both print
and ebook formats, contact booksales@hbr.org or visit www.hbr.org/bulksales.

The web addresses referenced in this book were live and correct at the time of the
book's publication but may be subject to change.

Cataloging-in-Publication data is forthcoming.

ISBN: 979-8-89279-302-5
eISBN: 979-8-89279-303-2

The paper used in this publication meets the requirements of the American National
Standard for Permanence of Paper for Publications and Documents in Libraries and
Archives Z39.48-1992.

Contents

HBR's 10 Must Reads

UPDATED &
EXPANDED

Innovation

1

What Is Disruptive Innovation?

by Clayton M. Christensen, Michael E. Raynor, and Rory McDonald

The theory of disruptive innovation, introduced in these pages in 1995, has proved to be a powerful way of thinking about innovation-driven growth. Many leaders of small, entrepreneurial companies praise it as their guiding star; so do many executives at large, well-established organizations, including Intel, Southern New Hampshire University, and Salesforce.com.

Unfortunately, disruption theory is in danger of becoming a victim of its own success. Despite broad dissemination, the theory's core concepts have been widely misunderstood and its basic tenets frequently misapplied. Furthermore, essential refinements in the theory over the past 20 years appear to have been overshadowed by the popularity of the initial formulation. As a result, the theory is sometimes criticized for shortcomings that have already been addressed.

There's another troubling concern: In our experience, too many people who speak of "disruption" have not read a serious book or article on the subject. Too frequently, they use the term loosely to invoke the concept of innovation in support of whatever it is they wish to do. Many researchers, writers, and consultants use "disruptive innovation" to describe *any* situation in which an industry is shaken up and previously successful incumbents stumble. But that's much too broad a usage.

The problem with conflating a disruptive innovation with any breakthrough that changes an industry's competitive patterns is that different types of innovation require different strategic approaches. To put it another way, the lessons we've learned about succeeding as a disruptive innovator (or defending against a disruptive challenger) will not apply to every company in a shifting market. If we get sloppy with our labels or fail to integrate insights from subsequent research and experience into the original theory, then managers may end up using the wrong tools for their context, reducing their chances of success. Over time, the theory's usefulness will be undermined.

This article is part of an effort to capture the state of the art. We begin by exploring the basic tenets of disruptive innovation and examining whether they apply to Uber. Then we point out some common pitfalls in the theory's application, how these arise, and why correctly using the theory matters. We go on to trace major turning points in the evolution of our thinking and make the case that what we have learned allows us to more accurately predict which businesses will grow.

First, a quick recap of the idea: "Disruption" describes a process whereby a smaller company with fewer resources is able to successfully challenge established incumbent businesses. Specifically, as incumbents focus on improving their products and services for

Idea in Brief

The Issue

The ideas summed up in the phrase "disruptive innovation" have become a powerful part of business thinking—but they're in danger of losing their usefulness because they've been misunderstood and misapplied.

The Response

The leading authorities on disruptive innovation revisit the central tenets of disruption theory, its development over the past 20 years, and its limitations.

The Bottom Line

Does it matter whether Uber, say, is a disruptive innovation or something else entirely? It does: We can't manage innovation effectively if we don't grasp its true nature.

their most demanding (and usually most profitable) customers, they exceed the needs of some segments and ignore the needs of others. Entrants that prove disruptive begin by successfully targeting those overlooked segments, gaining a foothold by delivering more-suitable functionality—frequently at a lower price. Incumbents, chasing higher profitability in more-demanding segments, tend not to respond vigorously. Entrants then move upmarket, delivering the performance that incumbents' mainstream customers require, while preserving the advantages that drove their early success. When mainstream customers start adopting the entrants' offerings in volume, disruption has occurred. (See the exhibit "The disruptive innovation model.")

Is Uber a Disruptive Innovation?

Let's consider Uber, the much-feted transportation company whose mobile application connects consumers who need rides with drivers who are willing to provide them. Founded in 2009, the company has enjoyed fantastic growth (it operates in hundreds of cities in 60 countries and is still expanding). It has reported tremendous financial success (the most recent funding round implies an enterprise value in the vicinity of $50 billion). And it has spawned a slew of imitators (other startups are trying to emulate its "market-making" business model). Uber is clearly transforming the taxi business in the United States. But is it *disrupting* the taxi business?

According to the theory, the answer is no. Uber's financial and strategic achievements do not qualify the company as genuinely disruptive—although the company is almost always described that way. Here are two reasons why the label doesn't fit.

Disruptive innovations originate in low-end or new-market footholds

Disruptive innovations are made possible because they get started in two types of markets that incumbents overlook. *Low-end footholds* exist because incumbents typically try to provide their most profitable and demanding customers with ever-improving products and services, and they pay less attention to less-demanding customers. In fact, incumbents' offerings often overshoot the performance requirements of the latter. This opens the door to a disrupter focused (at first) on providing those low-end customers with a "good enough" product.

In the case of *new-market footholds*, disrupters create a market where none existed. Put simply, they find a way to turn nonconsumers into consumers. For example, in the early days of photocopying technology, Xerox targeted large corporations and charged high prices in order to provide the performance that those customers required. School librarians, bowling-league operators, and other small customers, priced out of the market, made do

The disruptive innovation model

This diagram contrasts product performance trajectories *(the dashed lines showing how products or services improve over time) with* customer demand trajectories *(the solid lines showing customers' willingness to pay for performance). As incumbent companies introduce higher-quality products or services (upper dashed line) to satisfy the high end of the market (where profitability is highest), they overshoot the needs of low-end customers and many mainstream customers. This leaves an opening for entrants to find footholds in the less-profitable segments that incumbents are neglecting. Entrants on a disruptive trajectory (lower dashed line) improve the performance of their offerings and move upmarket (where profitability is highest for them, too) and challenge the dominance of the incumbents.*

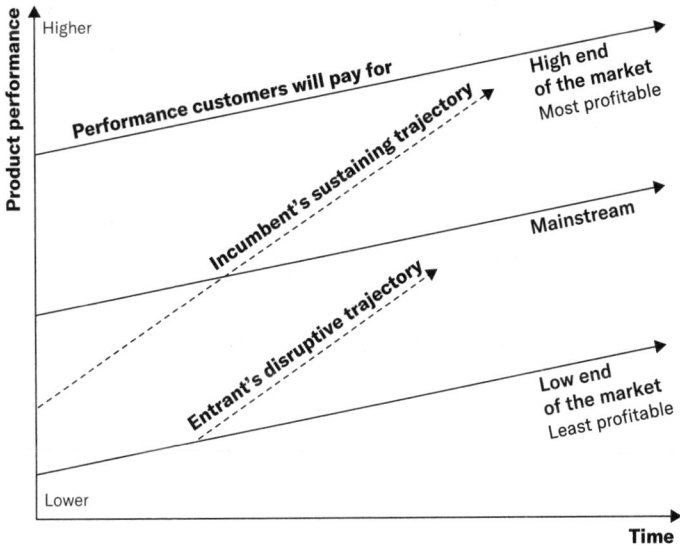

with carbon paper or mimeograph machines. Then in the late 1970s, new challengers introduced personal copiers, offering an affordable solution to individuals and small organizations—and a new market was created. From this relatively modest beginning, personal photocopier makers gradually built a major position in the mainstream photocopier market that Xerox valued.

A disruptive innovation, by definition, starts from one of those two footholds. But Uber did not originate in either one. It is difficult to claim that the company found a low-end opportunity: That would have meant taxi service providers had overshot the needs of a material number of customers by making cabs too plentiful, too easy to use, and too clean. Neither did Uber primarily target nonconsumers—people who found the existing alternatives so expensive or inconvenient that they took public transit or drove themselves instead: Uber was launched in San Francisco (a well-served taxi market), and Uber's customers were generally people already in the habit of hiring rides.

Uber has quite arguably been increasing total demand— that's what happens when you develop a better, less-expensive solution to a widespread customer need. But disrupters *start* by appealing to low-end or unserved consumers and then migrate to the mainstream market. Uber has gone in exactly the opposite direction: building a position in the mainstream market first and subsequently appealing to historically overlooked segments.

Disruptive innovations don't catch on with mainstream customers until quality catches up to their standards

Disruption theory differentiates disruptive innovations from what are called "sustaining innovations." The latter make good products better in the eyes of an incumbent's existing customers: the fifth blade in a razor, the clearer TV picture, better mobile phone reception. These improvements can be incremental advances or major breakthroughs, but they all enable firms to sell more products to their most profitable customers.

Disruptive innovations, on the other hand, are initially considered inferior by most of an incumbent's customers. Typically, customers are not willing to switch to the new offering merely because it is less expensive. Instead, they wait until its quality rises enough to satisfy them. Once that's happened, they adopt the new product and happily accept its lower price. (This is how disruption drives prices down in a market.)

Most of the elements of Uber's strategy seem to be sustaining innovations. Uber's service has rarely been described as inferior to existing taxis; in fact, many would say it is *better*. Booking a ride requires just a few taps on a smartphone; payment is cashless and convenient; and passengers can rate their rides afterward, which helps ensure high standards. Furthermore, Uber delivers service reliably and punctually, and its pricing is usually competitive with (or lower than) that of established taxi services. And as is typical when incumbents face threats from sustaining innovations, many of the taxi companies are motivated to respond. They are deploying competitive technologies, such as hailing apps, and contesting the legality of some of Uber's services.

Why Getting It Right Matters

Readers may still be wondering, Why does it matter what words we use to describe Uber? The company has certainly thrown the taxi industry into disarray: Isn't that "disruptive" enough? No. Applying the theory correctly is essential to realizing its benefits. For example, small competitors that nibble away at the periphery of your business very likely should be ignored— unless they are on a disruptive trajectory, in which case they are a potentially mortal threat. And both of these challenges are fundamentally different from efforts by competitors to woo your bread-and-butter customers.

As the example of Uber shows, identifying true disruptive innovation is tricky. Yet even executives with a good understanding of disruption theory tend to forget some of its subtler aspects when making strategic decisions. We've observed four important points that get overlooked or misunderstood:

1. Disruption is a process

The term "disruptive innovation" is misleading when it is used to refer to a product or service at one fixed point, rather than to the evolution of that product or service over time. The first minicomputers were disruptive not merely because they were low-end upstarts when they appeared on the scene, nor because they were later heralded as superior to mainframes in many markets; they were disruptive by virtue of the path they followed from the fringe to the mainstream.

Most every innovation—disruptive or not—begins life as a small-scale experiment. Disrupters tend to focus on getting the business model, rather than merely the product, just right. When they succeed, their movement from the fringe (the low end of the market or a new market) to the mainstream erodes first the incumbents' market share and then their profitability. This process can take time, and incumbents can get quite creative in the defense of their established franchises. For example, more than 50 years after the first discount department store was opened, mainstream retail companies still operate their traditional department-store formats. Complete substitution, if it comes at all, may take decades, because the incremental profit from staying with the old model for one more year trumps proposals to write off the assets in one stroke.

The fact that disruption can take time helps to explain why incumbents frequently overlook disrupters. For example, when Netflix launched, in 1997, its initial service wasn't appealing to most of Blockbuster's customers, who rented movies (typically new releases) on impulse. Netflix had an exclusively online interface and a large inventory of movies, but delivery through the U.S. mail meant selections took several days to arrive. The service appealed to only a few customer groups—movie buffs who didn't care about new releases, early adopters of DVD players, and online shoppers. If Netflix had not eventually begun to serve a broader segment of the market, Blockbuster's decision to ignore this competitor would not have been a strategic blunder: The two companies filled very different needs for their (different) customers.

However, as new technologies allowed Netflix to shift to streaming video over the internet, the company did eventually become appealing to Blockbuster's core customers, offering a wider selection of content with an all-you-can-watch, on-demand, low-price, high-quality, highly convenient approach. And it got there via a classically disruptive path. If Netflix (like Uber) had begun by launching a service targeted at a larger competitor's core market, Blockbuster's response would very likely have been a vigorous and perhaps successful counterattack. But failing to respond effectively to the trajectory that Netflix was on led Blockbuster to collapse.

2. Disrupters often build business models that are very different from those of incumbents

Consider the health care industry. General practitioners operating out of their offices often rely on their years of experience and on test results to interpret patients' symptoms, make diagnoses, and prescribe treatment. We call this a "solution shop" business model. In contrast, a number of convenient care clinics are taking a disruptive path by using what we call a "process" business model: They follow standardized protocols to diagnose and treat a small but increasing number of disorders.

One high-profile example of using an innovative business model to effect a disruption is Apple's iPhone. The product that Apple debuted in 2007 was a sustaining innovation in the smartphone market: It targeted the same customers coveted by incumbents, and its initial success is likely explained by product superiority. The iPhone's subsequent growth is better explained by disruption—not of other smartphones but of the laptop as the primary access point to the internet. This was achieved not merely through product improvements but also through the introduction of a new business model. By building a facilitated network connecting application developers with phone users, Apple changed the game. The iPhone created a new market for internet access and eventually was able to challenge laptops as mainstream users' device of choice for going online.

3. Some disruptive innovations succeed; some don't

A third common mistake is to focus on the results achieved—to claim that a company is disruptive by virtue of its success. But success is not built into the definition of disruption: Not every disruptive path leads to a triumph, and not every triumphant newcomer follows a disruptive path.

For example, any number of internet-based retailers pursued disruptive paths in the late 1990s, but only a small number prospered. The failures are not evidence of the deficiencies of disruption theory; they are simply boundary markers for the theory's application. The theory says very little about how to win in the foothold market, other than to play the odds and avoid head-on competition with better-resourced incumbents.

If we call every business success a "disruption," then companies that rise to the top in very different ways will be seen as sources of insight into a common strategy for succeeding. This creates a danger: Managers may mix and match behaviors that are very likely inconsistent with one another and thus unlikely to yield the hoped-for result. For example, both Uber and Apple's iPhone owe their success to a platform-based model: Uber digitally connects riders with drivers; the iPhone connects app developers with phone users. But Uber, true to its nature as a sustaining innovation, has focused on expanding its network and functionality in ways that make it better than traditional taxis. Apple, on the other hand, has followed a disruptive path by building its ecosystem of app developers so as to make the iPhone more like a personal computer.

4. The mantra "Disrupt or be disrupted" can misguide us

Incumbent companies do need to respond to disruption if it's occurring, but they should not overreact by dismantling a still-profitable business. Instead, they should continue to strengthen relationships with core customers by investing in sustaining innovations. In addition, they can create a new division focused solely on the growth opportunities that arise from the disruption. Our research suggests that the success of this new enterprise depends in large part on keeping it separate from the core business. That means that for some time, incumbents will find themselves managing two very different operations.

Of course, as the disruptive stand-alone business grows, it may eventually steal customers from the core. But corporate leaders should not try to solve this problem before it *is* a problem.

What a Disruptive Innovation Lens Can Reveal

It is rare that a technology or product is inherently sustaining or disruptive. And when new technology is developed, disruption theory does not dictate what managers should do. Instead it helps them make a strategic choice between taking a sustaining path and taking a disruptive one.

The theory of disruption predicts that when an entrant tackles incumbent competitors head-on, offering better products or services, the incumbents will accelerate their innovations to defend their business. Either they will beat back the entrant by offering even better services or products at comparable prices, or one of them will acquire the entrant. The data supports the theory's prediction that entrants pursuing a sustaining strategy for a stand-alone business will face steep odds: in Christensen's seminal study of the disk drive industry, only 6% of sustaining entrants managed to succeed.

Uber's strong performance therefore warrants explanation. According to disruption theory, Uber is an outlier, and we do not have a universal way to account for such atypical outcomes. In Uber's case, we believe that the regulated nature of the taxi business is a large part of the answer. Market entry and prices are closely controlled in many jurisdictions. Consequently, taxi companies have rarely innovated. Individual drivers have few ways to innovate, except to defect to Uber. So Uber is in a unique situation relative to taxis: it can offer better quality and the competition will find it hard to respond, at least in the short term.

To this point, we've addressed only whether or not Uber is disruptive to the taxi business. The limousine or "black car" business is a different story, and here Uber is far more likely to be on a disruptive path. The company's UberSELECT option provides more-luxurious cars and is typically more expensive than its standard service—but typically less expensive than hiring a traditional limousine. This lower price imposes some compromises, as UberSELECT currently does not include one defining feature of the leading incumbents in this market: acceptance

The ubiquitous "disruptive innovation"

"Disruptive innovation" and "disruptive technology" are now part of the popular business lexicon, as suggested by the dramatic growth in the number of articles using those phrases in recent years.

Articles

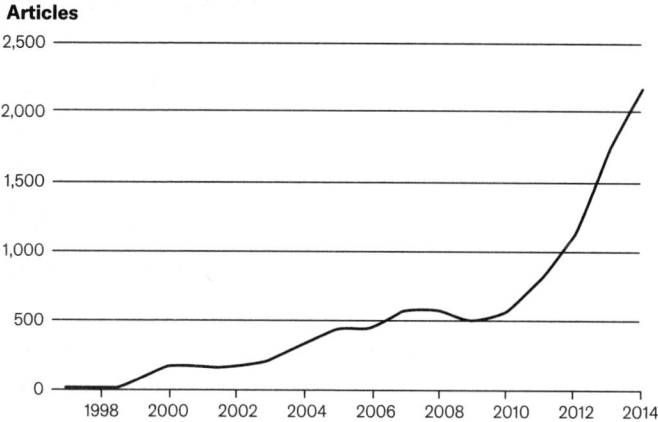

Source: Factiva analysis of a wide variety of English-language publications.

of advance reservations. Consequently, this offering from Uber appeals to the low end of the limousine service market: customers willing to sacrifice a measure of convenience for monetary savings. Should Uber find ways to match or exceed incumbents' performance levels without compromising its cost and price advantage, the company appears to be well positioned to move into the mainstream of the limo business—and it will have done so in classically disruptive fashion.

How Our Thinking About Disruption Has Developed

Initially, the theory of disruptive innovation was simply a statement about correlation. Empirical findings showed that incumbents outperformed entrants in a sustaining innovation context but underperformed in a disruptive innovation context. The reason for this correlation was not immediately evident, but one by one, the elements of the theory fell into place.

First, researchers realized that a company's propensity for strategic change is profoundly affected by the interests of customers who provide the resources the firm needs to survive. In other words, incumbents (sensibly) listen to their existing customers and concentrate on sustaining innovations as a result.

Researchers then arrived at a second insight: Incumbents' focus on their existing customers becomes institutionalized in internal processes that make it difficult for even senior managers to shift investment to disruptive innovations. For example, interviews with managers of established companies in the disk drive industry revealed that resource allocation processes prioritized sustaining innovations (which had high margins and targeted large markets with well-known customers) while inadvertently starving disruptive innovations (meant for smaller markets with poorly defined customers).

Those two insights helped explain why incumbents rarely responded effectively (if at all) to disruptive innovations, but not why entrants eventually moved upmarket to challenge incumbents, over and over again. It turns out, however, that the same forces leading incumbents to ignore early-stage disruptions also compel disrupters ultimately to disrupt.

What we've realized is that, very often, low-end and new-market footholds are populated not by a lone would-be disrupter, but by several comparable entrant firms whose products are simpler, more convenient, or less costly than those sold by incumbents. The incumbents provide a de facto price umbrella, allowing many of the entrants to enjoy profitable growth within the foothold market. But that lasts only for a time: As incumbents (rationally, but mistakenly) cede the foothold market, they effectively remove the price umbrella, and price-based competition among the entrants reigns. Some entrants will founder, but the smart ones—the true disrupters—will improve their products and drive upmarket, where, once again, they can compete at the margin against higher-cost established competitors. The disruptive effect drives every competitor—incumbent and entrant—upmarket.

With those explanations in hand, the theory of disruptive innovation went beyond simple correlation to a theory of causation as well. The key elements of that theory have been tested and validated through studies of many industries, including retail, computers, printing, motorcycles, cars, semiconductors, cardiovascular surgery, management education, financial services, management consulting, cameras, communications, and computer-aided design software.

Making sense of anomalies

Additional refinements to the theory have been made to address certain anomalies, or unexpected scenarios, that the theory could not explain. For example, we originally assumed that any disruptive innovation took root in the lowest tiers of an established market—yet sometimes new entrants seemed to be competing in entirely new markets. This led to the distinction we discussed earlier between low-end and new-market footholds.

Low-end disrupters (think steel minimills and discount retailers) come in at the bottom of the market and take hold within an existing value network before moving upmarket and attacking that stratum (think integrated steel mills and traditional retailers). By contrast, new-market disruptions take hold in a completely new value network and appeal to customers who have previously gone without the product. Consider the transistor pocket radio and the PC: They were largely ignored by manufacturers of tabletop radios and minicomputers, respectively, because they were aimed at nonconsumers of those goods. By postulating that there are two flavors of foothold markets in which disruptive innovation can begin, the theory has become more powerful and practicable.

Another intriguing anomaly was the identification of industries that have resisted the forces of disruption, at least until very recently. Higher education in the United States is one of these. Over the years—indeed, over more than 100 years—new kinds of institutions with different initial charters have been created to address the needs of various population segments, including nonconsumers. Land-grant universities, teachers' colleges, two-year colleges, and so on were initially launched to serve those for whom a traditional four-year liberal arts education was out of reach or unnecessary.

Many of these new entrants strived to improve over time, compelled by analogues of the pursuit of profitability: a desire for growth, prestige, and the capacity to do greater good. Thus they made costly investments in research, dormitories, athletic facilities, faculty, and so on, seeking to emulate more-elite institutions. Doing so has increased their level of performance in some ways—they can provide richer learning and living environments for students, for example. Yet the *relative* standing of higher-education institutions remains largely unchanged: With few exceptions, the top 20 are still the top 20, and the next 50 are still in that second tier, decade after decade.

Because both incumbents and newcomers are seemingly following the same game plan, it is perhaps no surprise that incumbents are able to maintain their positions. What has been missing—until recently—is experimentation with new models that successfully appeal to today's nonconsumers of higher education.

The question now is whether there is a novel technology or business model that allows new entrants to move upmarket without emulating the incumbents' high costs—that is, to follow a disruptive path. The answer seems to be yes, and the enabling innovation is online learning, which is becoming broadly available. Real tuition for online courses is falling, and accessibility and quality are improving. Innovators are making inroads into the mainstream market at a stunning pace.

Will online education disrupt the incumbents' model? And if so, when? In other words, will online education's trajectory of improvement intersect with the needs of the mainstream market? We've come to realize that the steepness of any disruptive trajectory is a function of how quickly the enabling technology improves. In the steel industry, continuous-casting technology improved quite slowly, and it took more than 40 years before the minimill Nucor matched the revenue of the largest integrated steelmakers. In contrast, the digital technologies that allowed personal computers to disrupt minicomputers improved much more quickly; Compaq was able to increase revenue more than tenfold and reach parity with the industry leader, DEC, in only 12 years.

Understanding what drives the rate of disruption is helpful for predicting outcomes, but it doesn't alter the way disruptions should be managed. Rapid disruptions are not fundamentally different from any others; they don't have different causal mechanisms and don't require conceptually different responses.

Similarly, it is a mistake to assume that the strategies adopted by some high-profile entrants constitute a special kind of disruption. Often these are simply miscategorized. Tesla Motors is a current and salient example. One might be tempted to say the company is disruptive. But its foothold is in the high end of the auto market (with customers willing to spend $70,000 or more on a car), and this segment is not uninteresting to incumbents. Tesla's entry, not surprisingly, has elicited significant attention and investment from established competitors. If disruption theory is correct, Tesla's future holds either acquisition by a much larger incumbent or a years-long and hard-fought battle for market significance.

We still have a lot to learn

We are eager to keep expanding and refining the theory of disruptive innovation, and much work lies ahead. For example, universally effective responses to disruptive threats remain elusive. Our current belief is that companies should create a separate division that operates under the protection of senior leadership to explore and exploit a new disruptive model. Sometimes this works—and sometimes it doesn't. In certain cases, a failed response to a disruptive threat cannot be attributed to a lack of understanding, insufficient executive attention, or inadequate financial investment. The challenges that arise from being an incumbent and an entrant simultaneously have yet to be fully specified; how best to meet those challenges is still to be discovered.

Disruption theory does not, and never will, explain everything about innovation specifically or business success generally. Far too many other forces are in play, each of which will reward further study. Integrating them all into a comprehensive theory of business success is an ambitious goal, one we are unlikely to attain anytime soon.

But there is cause for hope: Empirical tests show that using disruptive theory makes us measurably and significantly more accurate in our predictions of which fledgling businesses will succeed. As an ever-growing community of researchers and practitioners continues to build on disruption theory and integrate it with other perspectives, we will come to an even better understanding of what helps firms innovate successfully.

Originally published in December 2015. Reprint R1512B

2

Innovation Doesn't Have to Be Disruptive

by W. Chan Kim and Renée Mauborgne

The era of international travel began in the mid-19th century, with the golden age of transatlantic ocean-going. The British company Cunard, a leader in the industry, transported millions of immigrants from Europe to the United States around the turn of the 20th century. By the end of World War II it had emerged as the largest Atlantic passenger line, operating 12 ships to the United States and Canada as it captured the flourishing North Atlantic travel market in the first postwar decade.

That golden age came to an end with the advent of commercial jet flights. Whereas 1 million passengers crossed the Atlantic by boat in 1957, air travel caused that figure to fall to 650,000

Editor's Note: W. Chan Kim and Renée Mauborgne are the authors of *Beyond Disruption: Innovate and Achieve Growth Without Displacing Industries, Companies, or Jobs* (Harvard Business Review Press, 2023), from which this article is adapted.

by 1965, with roughly six people flying for each passenger going by sea. Ocean liners simply could not match the speed and convenience of jet planes.

But while other oceangoing companies were destroyed by the advent of the jet age, Cunard innovated "luxury vacationing at sea" and opened up the modern cruise industry. Until then ocean liners, like airplanes, had been viewed principally as a mode of transportation from point A to point B. Cunard changed that by making them platforms for recreation and star-studded entertainment.

Today Cunard is part of Carnival Corporation, and the cruise tourism industry it pioneered some 60 years ago generates revenues of about $30 billion annually and has created more than a million jobs. The creation of the cruise industry was clearly not incremental. Nor was it *disruptive*—the catchword that has come to dominate the innovation space. On the contrary, cruise tourism did not invade, destroy, or displace any existing market or industry. It was created *without disruption.*

An Alternative Path to Innovation and Growth

For the past 20 years "disruption" has been a leading battle cry in business: Disrupt this. Disrupt that. Disrupt or die. Whether it comes from the low end—the basis of Clay Christensen's theory of disruptive innovation—or from the high end, the way commercial jet travel overtook ocean liners and Apple's iPhone dominated mobile phones, corporate leaders have continually been told that the only way to innovate and grow is to disrupt their industries or even their own companies. Not surprisingly, many have come to see "disruption" as a near-synonym for "innovation."

Idea in Brief

The Problem

Innovation driven by disruption generates a new market and growth, but often with terrible social costs: the destruction of existing companies and jobs and damage to communities.

The Explanation

Most innovators have taken for granted that the surest path to growth is creating a new market by destroying the existing one. That overlooks an alternative approach to innovation that doesn't disrupt the existing industry.

The Solution

Nondisruptive creation occurs outside the boundaries of existing industries, giving rise to markets where none existed before. Thus it fosters economic growth without incurring social costs, enabling business and society to thrive together.

But the obsession with disruption obscures an important truth: Market-creating innovation isn't always disruptive. Disruption may be what people talk about. It's certainly important, and it's all around us. But as our research and the case of Cunard reveal, it's only one end of what we think of as the spectrum of market-creating innovation. On the other end is what we have come to call *nondisruptive creation,* through which new industries, new jobs, and profitable growth come into being without destroying existing companies or jobs.

Under disruption and its conceptual antecedent, Joseph Schumpeter's "creative destruction," market creation is inextricably linked to destruction or displacement. But nondisruptive creation breaks that link. It reveals an immense potential to establish markets where none existed before and, in doing so, to foster economic growth in a way that enables business and society to thrive together. In this article we will show how nondisruptive creation can complement disruption by offering an alternative path to market-creating innovation. We'll begin with the significant impact it can have on growth, jobs, and society.

Three Ideas That Changed the World

Today most women in developed countries take sanitary napkins for granted, but that one innovation created a nondisruptive new market that has radically improved the lives of half the world's population. Every month women use them to deal with the inconvenience (and messiness) of their menstrual cycles. But that wasn't always the case. Before the advent of sanitary napkins, women used pieces of old cloth or even sheep's wool, which were often dirty and could cause infection. They were uncomfortable, shifted when worn, and failed to prevent visible spotting and leakage. To avoid the embarrassment this caused, girls frequently stayed away from school for several days during their monthly cycles. Sanitary napkins took much of the stigma and dread out of menstruation: Girls could go to school and play sports without worry, and women could more easily work. Today the sanitary-napkin industry generates revenues of more than $22 billion a year.

Consider microfinance, an innovation that has transformed the lives of many of the world's poorest people by making financial services available to those who subsist on less than a few dollars a day. Before the advent of microfinance, no bank or other financial institution was prepared to serve them, deeming them unsuitable as borrowers. By finding a way around that problem, Muhammad Yunus, the founder of Grameen Bank, enabled people who had previously been denied access to capital to create new microbusinesses, jobs, higher standards of living, and hope. Microfinance has become a multibillion-dollar industry with a staggering 98% loan-repayment rate and plenty of room for future growth.

Now consider the television program *Sesame Street*, which teaches preschool children how to count, name colors and shapes, and recognize the letters of the alphabet. The best part is that kids have so much fun watching it, with its lovable Muppets and songs, that they don't even realize how much they're learning. *Sesame Street* did not displace preschools, libraries, or even parents who were reading bedtime stories to their children. Rather, it gave rise to a new industry—preschool edutainment—that for the most part had not existed before. Today it is a multibillion-dollar industry. And *Sesame Street* has become the most successful, longest-running children's television show in history, winning scores of Emmy Awards and 11 Grammys. It has viewers in more than 150 countries.

Although those three cases are disparate, they are all examples of nondisruptive creation. As our book *Beyond Disruption* shows, there are many others, in fields as diverse as cybersecurity, men's cosmeceuticals, environmental consulting, life coaching, pharmaceuticals, and smartphone accessories—not to mention the emerging space tourism industry led by companies such as Virgin Galactic, SpaceX, and Blue Origin. All those have created or are creating new multibillion-dollar industries, growth, and employment, without displacing any existing markets, players, or jobs.

A Distinct New Concept

From the examples we've just presented and the others we've studied, we've identified three fundamental characteristics of nondisruptive creation. First, it can occur with either new or

From Blue Ocean Strategy to Nondisruptive Creation

After the publication of our books *Blue Ocean Strategy* and *Blue Ocean Shift*, a question repeatedly popped up from business leaders, academics, and consultants working in the field of innovation: **How does blue ocean strategy differ from creative destruction, disruption, or disruptive innovation?**

To address that question, we reexamined our blue ocean data from the innovation angle and found that although a few cases, such as Novo Nordisk's insulin pen, largely displaced the existing offerings in their own industries, most blue oceans in our data were created not *within* existing industry boundaries but *across* them. Cirque du Soleil, for instance, created a new market space across the existing boundaries of circus and theater. Although it pulled some market share from both, generating a measure of disruption, it did not significantly displace either.

However, our examination also revealed something else that greatly intrigued us. Among the cases that had been added to our original database over time, a few had triggered no disruption or displacement. That piqued our curiosity. Did those cases represent a few unconnected anomalies, or were they examples of a new kind of innovation? If the latter, why had it been largely overlooked in the literature on innovation and growth? What were its implications for business and society, now and in the future? And was there a process or an approach by which we could realize

existing technology. It may stem from a scientific invention or a technology-driven innovation, as sanitary pads and space tourism did. But it can also be generated *without* such innovation, as was the case with microfinance, or with a new combination or application of existing technology, as with *Sesame Street,* which leveraged television.

this new kind of innovation in a systematic way? To answer those questions we collected historical and current cases of nondisruptive creation across the for-profit, nonprofit, and public sectors and built a database on nondisruptive creation and the managerial actions involved in it.

Our research showed that nondisruptive creation is distinct from both disruption and blue ocean strategy, with a correspondingly distinct impact on growth. Whereas disruption generates new markets *within* existing industry boundaries, resulting in a high level of disruptive growth, and blue ocean strategy creates new markets *across* existing industry boundaries, producing a mix of disruptive and nondisruptive growth, nondisruptive creation generates new markets *outside* existing industry boundaries and yields mostly nondisruptive growth. Our book *Beyond Disruption* details our journey and offers the answers we found to the questions we asked.

For discussions on the existence and economic importance of new goods, including those that do not replace existing ones, see *The Economics of New Goods*, ed. T. Bresnahan and R. Gordon (Chicago: University of Chicago Press, 1996). Relatedly, Amar Bhidé discussed new goods that don't destroy existing ones and introduced the term *nondestructive creation*. Its conceptual characteristics and definition differ from those of *nondisruptive* creation referred to here; for his discussion, see Amar Bhidé, *The Venturesome Economy: How Innovation Sustains Prosperity in a More Connected World* (Princeton: Princeton University Press, 2008).

Second, nondisruptive creation is applicable across geographic areas, from developed markets to bottom-of-the-pyramid markets, and at all levels of socioeconomic standing. *Sesame Street* and sanitary pads were created in and initially for developed economies, while microfinance was created in and initially for the bottom of the pyramid. Cunard cruises were initially for people in the upper to middle tiers of socioeconomic standing, and microfinance was initially for the lower tier.

Third, nondisruptive creation can be new-to-the-world innovation, but the two are not equivalent. For one thing, many new-to-the-world innovations are disruptive, as commercial jet travel was to ocean liners. For another, nondisruptive creation can be new to an area but *not* new to the world. Take Ping An Good Doctor, which built a nondisruptive market of primary health care in China. No such service had existed there before, whereas the West, for example, already had a primary care market.

What all this means is that nondisruptive creation is not the same as—nor should it be confused with—scientific invention or technological innovation or new-to-the-world products or services. Nor is it concerned with a specific geographic market, such as the bottom of the pyramid, or a certain socioeconomic level, such as the low end. It is distinct from existing innovation concepts and can be defined as "the creation of a brand-new market *beyond the boundaries* of existing industries." That means that no existing market or established players are disrupted and fail, and no jobs are lost. (For a discussion of our research on this, see the sidebar "From Blue Ocean Strategy to Nondisruptive Creation.")

How the Economic and Social Impacts Differ

Consider these examples: Netflix versus Blockbuster, Amazon versus booksellers and Main Street retailers, and Uber versus taxis. They come from different industries, but they have three key factors in common: They're all cases of disruption. They all reflect a clear win-lose situation. And they all impose painful adjustment costs on society. Let's explore this.

On the positive side, consumers win big-time. That's why people gravitate to disruptive offerings. For a product or a service to disrupt, it must deliver a leap in value (typically underscored by a new business model); otherwise the industry won't be thrown into disarray, and purchasers, whether they be businesses or consumers, will see no reason to shift from the incumbent offering to the new one.

In economic terms we can say that the consumer surplus delivered by the disrupter is high, and society's resources are allocated where they are deemed to be better used. That's why disruption tends to grow industries as well as upend them: The compelling value it unlocks draws people who didn't previously purchase incumbents' products or services, and it inspires incumbents' existing customers to use the new offerings more frequently. For example, more people watch Netflix than used to rent DVDs from Blockbuster, and more people take digital photos than ever took photos with film—just as more people cross the ocean in planes than ever did on ocean liners, and with greater frequency.

But growth here is achieved in a win-lose way. The disrupter's success comes at the direct expense of existing players and markets. Which brings us to the second commonality: Disruption imposes a clear trade-off between winners and losers. In some cases one wins and everyone else loses. That's because the leap in consumer surplus provided by the disrupter can nearly wipe out the existing industry and its incumbent players. Amazon didn't merely displace Borders' 1,200 stores, along with countless independent booksellers, and take a huge chunk out of Barnes & Noble's sales. It is now doing the same to Main Street retailers and department stores in the United States and other countries it operates in.

Although the disrupter is hailed as a winner in the press, and purchasers and investors flock to it, this win-lose approach triggers the third commonality: painful adjustment costs for society, often hidden by the euphoria and glamour that surround disruption. For example, in New York City, Uber's largest U.S. market, the company has had a huge impact on taxi drivers and medallion owners who bought the right to operate a taxi in the city. Long seen as a retirement ticket, taxi medallions have plunged in value from more than $1 million to as little as $175,000 since the appearance of Uber and other ride-hailing services, and taxi drivers' earnings have nosedived by as much as 40%. Many drivers must now work double shifts just to survive. Bankruptcies, foreclosures, evictions, and even suicides have resulted. Such negative aftershocks are felt worldwide in major cities that Uber and similar services have entered. The same disruptive force that has enriched consumers with its leap in value has hurt others in the process. The human costs of Amazon's disruption are even more pronounced: Retail jobs may not be glamorous, but they provide a livelihood for millions of people. And the visual effect of boarded-up stores wears on people's psyches and tarnishes a community.

In theory, disruption should generate higher growth and new jobs, but painful adjustment costs exist in the short run. For example, Amazon's disruption of booksellers and retail has led to as many as 900,000 jobs lost and huge existing-asset obsolescence. And although Amazon's workforce had climbed from 200,000 to 800,000 when Covid hit, and its net positive impact on jobs and growth has increased since, the jobs it is creating are not necessarily located where the old jobs were lost and may not rest on the same skills and knowledge as those of the workers let go. People who were laid off may still be reeling, especially if they're in rural communities where local jobs were scarce to begin with.

Disruption vs. nondisruptive creation

The impact of nondisruptive creation can be distinguished from that of disruption at three levels. The micro level focuses on individual organizations, the meso level on groups or their interactions, and the macro level on the economy or society.

Level	Disruption	Nondisruptive creation
Micro	→ Generates growth through the displacement and expansion of existing market space	→ Generates growth through the creation of new market space beyond existing industries
Meso	→ Produces a win-lose outcome **Winners:** the disrupter and consumers **Losers:** disrupted organizations and their employees	→ Produces a positive-sum outcome **Winners:** the nondisruptive creator and consumers **Losers:** none evident
Macro	→ Incurs social adjustment costs from shuttered organizations, lost jobs, and hurt communities → Short-term growth comes with social pain, although the *net* gain in growth over time is positive	→ Incurs no evident social adjustment costs because there is no displacement → The gains in economic growth and employment are positive from the start, with no social pain

Even though, at the macro level, disruption yields aggregate long-run growth, the ensuing adjustment costs often trigger a backlash from social interest groups, government agencies, and nonprofit associations seeking to minimize the carnage. (Of course, if an industry has a pronounced negative effect on the environment or the well-being of people, the trade-off may be small relative to the overall benefit to society of disrupting and displacing that industry.)

Adjustment costs are where nondisruptive creation breaks from disruption. By effectively disentangling market creation from market destruction, it allows organizations to grow with little asset obsolescence and social pain. All else being equal, it can be seen as a positive-sum approach to innovation—a much-needed complement to disruption as a pathway to growth. Let's explore that idea.

Toward a Positive-Sum Outcome

Like disruption, nondisruptive creation delivers compelling value for buyers, whether they are consumers or businesses. That's why we purchase or use the product or service, and the new market materializes. Without exceptional value, the new market will not take off. In contrast to disruption, however, nondisruptive creation produces no evident losers and only minimal painful adjustment costs. From the start it has a positive impact on growth and jobs.

Kickstarter, for example, saw that literally thousands of people had wildly imaginative projects they dreamed of creating but lacked the capital to pursue. Because most artists are aiming first and foremost to realize a vision, not to generate ROI, it should come as no surprise that Kickstarter's online crowd-funding platform didn't eat into the existing finance industry or displace even a tiny share of existing equity investors' or venture capitalists' profits, growth, or investment opportunities. And because backers receive no monetary incentives on Kickstarter—only cool merchandise or other recognition, such as a shout-out on the creative's website—a new set of investors emerged: people who care about creative work and want to help others realize their dreams.

Hailed after its launch as one of *Time* magazine's 50 best inventions of the year, Kickstarter succeeded while creating few if any losers. Within three years of its advent it became profitable, and in its first decade it raised a staggering $4.3 billion for projects supported on its platform, funding more than 160,000 ideas that might have gone unrealized otherwise. According to a study at the University of Pennsylvania, Kickstarter estimates that more than 300,000 part-time and full-time jobs were created by its projects, along with 8,800 new companies and nonprofits, generating more than $5.3 billion in direct economic impact for those creators and their communities. No one lost a job because of Kickstarter, and no company went out of business because of it. It helped the artistic community flourish without unleashing hurt or painful adjustment costs. That was pretty much a win all around.

The Rising Importance of Nondisruptive Creation

Ever since the Nobel Prize–winning economist Milton Friedman introduced his theory of shareholder primacy, there has been a presumed trade-off between maximizing economic gain and social good. Friedman's theory, which is at the heart of capitalism as we know it today, asserts that "there is one and only one social responsibility of business—to use its resources and engage in activities designed to increase its profits." Social issues beyond that fall outside the proper scope of the enterprise.

Yet for all the economic benefits this approach has brought, it is increasingly being challenged as the world wakes up to the costly social effects that result from the pursuit of profit maximization. And the public is becoming increasingly vocal about them, demanding that corporations expand their mission beyond profit and consider the impact of their actions on local communities and society at large. The result is an increase in discussions about the need for a socially responsible form of capitalism. Nondisruptive creation speaks to this, not by compromising economic good but by innovating new markets without destruction.

The influence of the fourth industrial revolution also underscores nondisruptive creation's growing importance for the future. AI, smart machines, and robotics are on track to deliver previously unimaginable efficiencies, but they will do so by replacing an increasingly wide swath of existing human jobs. Studies show that smart machines are expected to displace about 20 million manufacturing jobs worldwide over the next decade, more than 1.5 million of them in the United States. Other studies predict that smart machines, robotics, artificial intelligence, blockchain technology, 3D printing, and automation will put 20% to 40% of existing jobs at risk over the coming decades, including a range of high-end jobs across most sectors, from medical to legal, finance, real estate, and journalism. And as recent advances show, AI is even capable of creating beautiful original art and music.

To absorb all the released human capital, new jobs will be needed—which brings us right back to the central driver of economic growth: market-creating innovation. The success of technology and the productivity it unleashes raise the premium on creativity and the establishment of new markets. The challenge for companies, governments, and society will be to create new jobs that don't displace others. That is as much an economic imperative as it is a moral one—which is another reason why nondisruptive creation is about to become even more important. Microfinance has given nearly 140 million people loans to start microenterprises and be gainfully self-employed. Life coaching, another nondisruptive industry, is estimated to have created tens of thousands of new jobs. Environmental consulting has given rise to thousands of new jobs, and that number will no doubt grow as public concern mounts over environmental degradation. Nondisruptive creation is not the sole answer to the challenges we face; many other pieces of the puzzle are needed. But it should be part of any solution.

Identifying Nondisruptive Opportunities

So how can organizations go about finding and realizing opportunities for nondisruptive creation? To answer that question, we studied whether a pattern lies behind successful nondisruptive creations—and if so, what it looks like. Our aim was to codify the recurring thought processes and actions of nondisruptive creators so that other organizations could use them for maximum effect.

Three building blocks are key to nondisruptive creation: Identifying a nondisruptive opportunity, finding a way to unlock it, and securing the enablers needed to realize it in a high-value, low-cost way. In this article, because of space limitations, we focus on the first one. There are two main ways to identify a nondisruptive opportunity.

Address an existing but unexplored issue or problem. Nondisruptive markets are created by solving a brand-new problem or uncovering a brand-new opportunity beyond existing industry boundaries. That doesn't necessarily mean that the problem or the opportunity suddenly popped up. It may have long existed but—importantly—has remained unexplored because it wasn't seen as a problem to solve or an opportunity for creation. Sometimes people have consciously or unconsciously accepted it as simply "the way things are." Sometimes a reputable organization or individuals may have tried long ago to address the issue and failed, so people regard it as essentially impossible. And sometimes it may be taken for granted and accepted because people have patched together some form of nonmarket solution to the problem—as women did before the creation of sanitary pads.

Take Square (now Block). Jim McKelvey and Jack Dorsey, the founders, saw that individuals and microbusinesses were losing sales because they couldn't accept credit card payments. That problem had long existed but had somehow been accepted as a natural struggle that goes hand in hand with running a small business. It was McKelvey's direct loss of a sale for his glassblowing business that highlighted this existing but unexplored problem and made the two men passionate about solving it as they realized how many would benefit from this new market, from small businesses to pop-up shops, ice cream trucks, and even babysitters. Square's solution, the Square Reader, created a nondisruptive new market. It had little if any effect on existing merchants and their credit card providers, and Square quickly grew into a billion-dollar company without facing any real backlash or fight from established players.

On a smaller scale, consider Mick Ebeling, Daniel Belquer, and their Not Impossible Labs. The fact that deaf people can't experience music had long been taken for granted as an unfortunate fact of life. Ebeling and Belquer, however, saw it not as the inevitable destiny of the deaf but as a brand-new opportunity to innovate. So they and the rest of the team at Not Impossible Labs set out to change things with Music: Not Impossible. They realized that although sound vibrations enter the brain through the ears, it is the brain that "hears." So to get vibrations to the brain, they used the skin instead of the ear, developing a wearable vibro-tactile device for deaf concertgoers—a vest, to be worn over a shirt, that contains a full sound system of 24 lightweight vibrators strategically placed at the waist, the neck, and the shoulders. The result was the world's first rock concert for deaf people. Music: Not Impossible is now scaling up the delivery of its offering across the globe, from a music festival in

London to an opera house in Philadelphia to the Brazilian Symphony Orchestra to silent discos at Lincoln Center, reaching out to the deaf and the hearing alike.

GoPro, Liquid Paper, Pfizer's Viagra, Prodigy Finance, and, going back in time, the humble but indispensable windshield wiper and the dishwasher are just a few more of the countless nondisruptive creations generated by tackling existing but unexplored issues and problems with market solutions.

Address a newly emerging issue or problem. Socioeconomic, environmental, demographic, and technological changes that have an impact on society or people's lives give rise to new problems, opportunities, and issues. Offering an effective market solution to an emerging need or opportunity—beyond existing industry boundaries—opens the door to a nondisruptive new market. Consider the Tongwei Group, a Chinese aquatic-feed producer. Mounting global pressure for clean, low-carbon energy created a new push in China for green sources of energy, especially in the eastern and central regions, where industrial activity was concentrated and power demand was rising. Those regions are densely populated, with rural land reserved for agricultural use, leaving scant space for green-energy production facilities.

Seeing this emerging need, the Tongwei Group set out to create a brand-new, nondisruptive market by leveraging its business, which serviced millions of acres of fish-farm waters in eastern and central China. Although aquaculture was already an important source of revenue for individual farmers and local governments, Tongwei determined that the economic value of those water resources could be multiplied by using the water's unutilized surface to produce green energy.

So the company created a nondisruptive, fishery-integrated, photovoltaic industry, which essentially combined an innovative cage-type aquacultural system that it had developed with a water-based photovoltaic system. Solar panels set above the water had the effect of lowering water temperatures and reducing photosynthesis and algal growth, which boosted the output of the fish farms. Meanwhile, Tongwei generated electricity with the solar panels. The results of this nondisruptive creation were higher incomes for fish farmers, a new source of green energy for the regions, more tax revenues for local governments, and a highly profitable new business for Tongwei. Tongwei's new market disrupts no one and is expanding rapidly across China.

Consider another nondisruptive market: e-sports. Youths had a fast-growing interest in watching skillful professionals play online video games, whether or not they were gamers themselves. In response, video-game makers and third-party e-sports organizers created professional in-person tournaments in which the most skilled players could compete in spectacular global events, held in massive arenas, with as many as 50,000 people in attendance and the players' moves projected on panoramic screens. They entered into lucrative agreements to broadcast the events live around the world, with up to 100 million fans watching. In this way e-sports was crafted into a spectator sport distinct from gaming itself. Today the industry pulls in more than $1 billion in revenue and has some 175 million fans worldwide. Its creation and growth have not displaced any existing gaming or other sports industries.

The relevant questions are: What taken-for-granted problems that no industry exists to solve do you or your company observe or directly experience? What newly emerging issues are you or your organization encountering that have no industry addressing them and could create a real opportunity for you, your business, or the world? Are you actively scouting brand-new problems to solve and brand-new opportunities for creation? Do you have a mechanism, a process, or tools for doing so effectively?

. . .

As we seek to address the many challenges facing our planet and humanity, we will need innovative market-creating solutions. If they can be nondisruptive rather than disruptive, we believe, they will help bridge the gap between business and society, bringing people together rather than dividing them.

Much of business is about aggression and fear: beating the competition, stealing market share, disrupting or being disrupted. Most of us dislike those emotions and behaviors because they fill us with anxiety, making us feel we are under threat and may be marginalized or destroyed if we don't strike first. It's a scarcity-based view of the world. What if we could shift from fear to hope, from a mindset of scarcity to one of abundance? The idea that we can create new markets and grow without disrupting others suggests that business does not have to be a destructive, fear-based, win-lose game.

To be sure, fear can be effective. "Disrupt or die" is a strong motivator for an organization to act. But the hope of making a positive-sum contribution to business and society is equally strong. That's why it's important to understand and act on both ends of the spectrum of market-creating innovation, and why nondisruptive creation is an essential complement to disruption. Each has a role to play in building a compelling future.

Originally published May–June 2023. Reprint R2303D

Great Innovators Create the Future, Manage the Present, and Selectively Forget the Past

by Vijay Govindarajan

For a long time, I have been troubled to see how often organizations fail to invest wisely in their futures while instead placing dominant emphasis on the present. To be sure, the present is vitally important. Your current business is the *performance engine*. It both funds day-to-day operations and generates profits for the future. Where problems arise is when the present crowds out other strategic priorities—for example, when the *only* skills brought into a business are those that serve today's core. That is shortsighted in every sense of the word.

What's missing from the managerial tool kit is a way for managers to allocate their—and their organization's—time and

---

Editor's Note: This text was excerpted from the Harvard Business Review Press book The Three-Box Solution: A Strategy for Leading Innovation *(2016).*

attention and resources on a day-to-day basis across the competing demands of managing both today's requirements and
tomorrow's possibilities. But as anyone who has ever tried to
lead innovation knows, the challenge goes beyond being ambi-
dextrous enough to manage today's business while creating
tomorrow's.[1] There is a third, and even more intractable, problem: not letting go of yesterday's values and beliefs that keep the
company stuck in the past.

To deal with this issue, over the course of 35 years of working
with and doing research in corporations around the world, I have
developed a simple, practical framework that recognizes all three
competing challenges managers face when leading innovation. It
is based on the simple idea that the future is not located on some
far-off horizon, and you cannot postpone the work of building
it until tomorrow. To get to the future, you must build it day by
day. That means being able to selectively set aside certain beliefs,
assumptions, and practices created in and by the past that would
otherwise become a rock wall between your business of today
and its future potential. This is the basic idea behind what I call
the Three-Box Solution (see the figure below).

Success in each box requires a different set of skills, attitudes,
practices, and leadership. By balancing the activities and behaviors associated with each box, every day, your organization will
be inventing the future as a steady process over time rather
than as a onetime, cataclysmic, do-or-die event. Simply put, the
future is shaped by what you do, and don't do, today.

The three-box framework will help you deliver stronger overall performance and more-innovative futures while also building
an organization fit to survive not just from quarter to quarter but
for generations. As Karim Tabbouche, the chief consumer officer of stc Bahrain, told me: "Our planning process had become

Idea in Brief

The Problem

Leaders often place too much emphasis on keeping today's business humming and fail to invest wisely in the future. Even more frequently, they don't *let go* of the values and beliefs that may have worked yesterday but are now holding them back.

How to Fix It

The Three-Box Solution provides a practical framework for resolving the inherent tensions of innovating while running a high-performing business at the same time. The trick is balancing the activities and behaviors associated with each box every day.
  Box 1: Manage the Present
  Box 2: Forget the Past
  Box 3: Create the Future

Beware the "Success Trap"

The biggest challenge you'll face in balancing the three boxes is that the more success you have with Box 1, the more difficult it will be to release what's worked in the past to conceive and execute Box 3 strategies. That's why Box 2 is the framework's most indispensable—but most often overlooked—element.

myopic and short term in nature, with our objectives becoming tactical and linear in nature. The three-box framework has challenged us to redesign the planning process, which would allow us to brainstorm Box 2 and Box 3 nonlinear initiatives in addition to undertaking Box 1 operational excellence initiatives. It is important to allocate resources to Box 1, Box 2, and Box 3 projects to maintain a healthy balance among the boxes."

Yet, it is not surprising that so many organizations focus mainly—even exclusively—on Box 1. The Box 1 present is their comfort zone, based on activities and ideas that are proven, well understood, and firmly embedded in the business. Most firms' organizational structures were built on the successes of the past,

The Three-Box Solution

By balancing the three boxes, managers can resolve the inherent tension of innovating a new business while running a high-performing business at the same time.

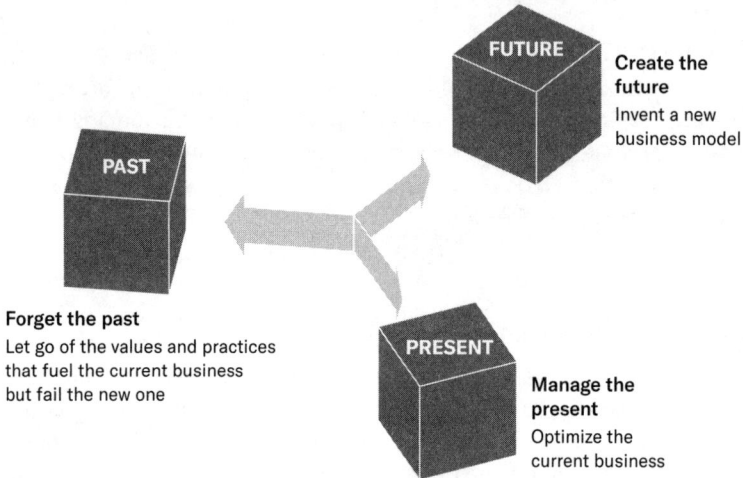

Create the future
Invent a new business model

Forget the past
Let go of the values and practices that fuel the current business but fail the new one

Manage the present
Optimize the current business

Source: Vijay Govindarajan, *The Three-Box Solution* (Harvard Business Review Press, 2016).

refined over time to support the priorities of the present core business, and focused on maximizing cash flow and profit generated by the core.

By comparison, the Box 2 work of avoiding the traps of the past is difficult and painful. It may require wrenching management decisions to divest long-standing lines of business or to abandon entrenched practices and attitudes that are unwelcoming or even hostile to ideas that don't conform to the dominant model of past success. Moreover, the Box 3 methodology for creating the future consists of leaps of faith and experimentation that are fraught with uncertainty and risk. The regime calls for entirely different management strategies and metrics than the relatively settled and predictable work of executing the present core business at the highest level does.

The biggest challenge you have in balancing the three boxes is that the greater your success in Box 1, the more difficulties you are likely to face in conceiving and executing breakthrough Box 3 strategies. This "success trap" typically arises not from willful inattention but from the overwhelming power of success that the past has brought.

For example, like most other forms of popular entertainment, Hasbro competes in a "hits based" industry, launching many new products in the hope that one or more will become the sort of breakout platform or franchise that vastly overcompensates for the cost of developing products that don't hit it big. Over the years, Hasbro has had its share of legendary hits (Mr. Potato Head, G.I. Joe, and Transformers), each becoming a growth platform. But until 20 years ago, the company had continued to see itself as a toy and game manufacturer for the retail channel.

The risk for a business of Hasbro's type is that it could become complacent, resting on its laurels and perhaps failing to notice changes in the environment that could threaten a formerly secure business model. That is why organizations must develop the Box 2 capacity to overcome the influence of the past, to divest one identity in favor of another.

Had Hasbro continued to see itself as a toy and game manufacturer whose customer relationships existed only at the retail point of sale, it would not be the successful company it is today. In the intervening decades, it transformed itself by shedding its old identities. That is among the many reasons why Box 2, whose mechanisms explicitly target success traps, is such an important enabler of Box 3 innovation.

With the three boxes in mind, here are the key takeaways that I find work best with managers trying to balance the competing demands of innovating while running a high-performing business:

Do not distract those who work in the core Box 1 business from their demanding performance goals. Box 1 cannot execute Box 3 innovations. And that is OK. Remember that Box 3 cannot exist without Box 1. Also, what must be forgotten for the purposes of Box 3 may still be vitally important to Box 1.

Box 2 is the indispensable element of the Three-Box Solution. Most organizations ignore Box 2 as they try to innovate their way to a new model. Even as old ideas and practices choke off the new future they're trying to create, organizations find it very difficult to overcome the power of the past. The more attention a company pays to Box 2, the more room there is for Box 3 to achieve its goals. If Box 3 were an NFL quarterback, Box 2 would be the offensive line, providing time and flexibility in which to read the defense, execute, and, if necessary, improvise. Without a well-functioning Box 2 discipline, your Box 3 offense will be stagnant and predictable.

Good Box 3 hedging strategies are important. In a regime of experimentation and learning, not every step along the way will be successful. You need to develop a process for hedging risk. That typically means testing assumptions through iterative learning stages that, over time, resolve uncertainty and either produce growing confidence or reveal the need for a reboot or exit. Hasbro's 1970s venture into *Romper Room*–branded nursery schools might have benefited from better testing and hedging.

Create formal processes that both serve the goals of Box 3 and increase the likelihood of achieving balance among all three boxes. Sustainable Box 3 activities require both structure and accountability. Former Hasbro CEO Brian Goldner inaugurated "martini meetings" and the Future Now team to keep Hasbro moving forward on Box 3 ideas. The martini meetings served the further purpose of identifying situations in which the three boxes might intersect. This became procedural reinforcement of the boxes' relatedness and ultimately contributed to balance. On a personal time-management level, Goldner audited the amount of attention he devoted to each box every week.

Think of the Three-Box Solution as endlessly cyclical. You are always preserving the present, destroying the past, and building the future. In other words, the business models, products, and services you create in Box 3 will at some point become your new Box 1.

The Three-Box Solution imposes on leaders a requirement for humility, because it is essentially a strategy for taking action through continuous learning. Learning is intrinsically a humbling activity; to learn is to admit you don't know everything. Almost every aspect of the Three-Box Solution framework is intended to increase opportunities to listen and learn. In my experience, the most effective leaders also happen to be good listeners, are never arrogant, and are able to disregard rank and status in the service of finding the best ideas.

The Three-Box Solution requires an ability to think and act simultaneously in multiple time frames. You're always managing the present, destroying the past, and building the future. At times, you will have to focus on one box more than the others, but if you attend to all three boxes with your teams and others in your organization, you will find that you're creating the future over time, every single day.

Adapted from hbr.org, March 31, 2016. Reprint H02R9L

3

A New Approach to Strategic Innovation

by Haijian Si, Christoph Loch, and Stelios Kavadias

Companies typically treat their innovation projects as a portfolio: a mix of projects that, collectively, aim to meet their various strategic objectives. Some projects, for instance, will improve business processes; others develop new products and services.

But while the portfolio concept can be helpful, our research suggests that portfolio objectives have become overly standardized. Most companies, in other words, seek similar portfolio objectives, such as achieving a balance between making incremental improvements and applying new technologies. All too often, executives carefully evaluate individual projects along standard performance metrics such as net present value, but they spend little time thinking about what types of projects the company's competitive positioning needs beyond the general notion—borrowed from finance—that diversification reduces risks. As a result, companies' innovation projects tend to be only weakly related to their distinctive strategic goals, and at worst, they work against its strategy.

When we surveyed 75 companies in China, we discovered that when executives took the trouble to link their project selection to their business's competitive goals, the contribution of their innovation activities to performance increased dramatically. This article introduces a strategic innovation tool kit we developed to help companies align their innovation investments with their unique competitive strategies. We tested the tool successfully across 10 business units at five companies.

Creating Strategic Alignment

Our tool kit is anchored in two graphics that, taken together, help companies relate their innovation projects to their strategic goals. Companies begin with an examination of their business strategy.

Achieving consensus and identifying strategic change needs

In almost half the companies we have worked with, members of the management team held varying understandings of their company's strategy. Our process is designed to get business unit leaders on the same page. We ask them to list their unit's strategic goals (for example, growth or profits) and succinctly characterize their business unit's strategy. For this, we use the widely known 3W1H (what, who, why, and how) framework, plus a fifth question on weaknesses, but other frameworks may also be used. Completing this exercise helps leaders articulate a shared view of their strategic position, which will enable them to reach the strategic goals.

Idea in Brief

The Problem

Companies typically treat their innovation projects as a portfolio, aiming for a mix that will collectively meet their strategic objectives. But too often, a company's innovation projects are only weakly related to its strategic goals, and at worst, they work against its strategy.

The Cause

Portfolio objectives often pursue a standardized balance, such as between making incremental improvements and applying new technologies, and projects are evaluated by customary criteria such as net present value or risk-return.

The Solution

A new tool helps leaders align innovation investments with their specific strategies. The tool may require a cultural shift, since it requires a more iterative way of making decisions.

The last question in our process identifies *change needs*. These change needs reflect weaknesses in the company's current strategic position (for example, "Our costs are too high," or "We are not addressing a key customer segment," or "Our competitors are coming out with a new product generation that will make our functionality insufficient"). These weaknesses often signal innovation opportunities; it's not coincidental that a widely accepted definition of innovation is "any deliberate change that helps the strategic position of the organization."

Creating the innovation basket

The process of categorizing innovation projects is the next step, and it is where our process deviates from established frameworks. We use the word "basket" rather than "portfolio" to denote a company's collection of innovation projects. In this

The strategic innovation tool kit

Our innovation tool kit consists of the strategy summary framework and the innovation basket. As leadership teams work through these exercises, they will gain consensus on strategy, identify threats and weaknesses, translate those weaknesses into innovation goals, and cultivate a collection of innovation projects that support their strategy. Evaluation of the basket may also trigger a change in strategy.

1 Using the what-who-why-how framework, management teams clarify their business unit's strategy. From there, they ask a fifth question: "What needs to change in order to achieve our strategy?"

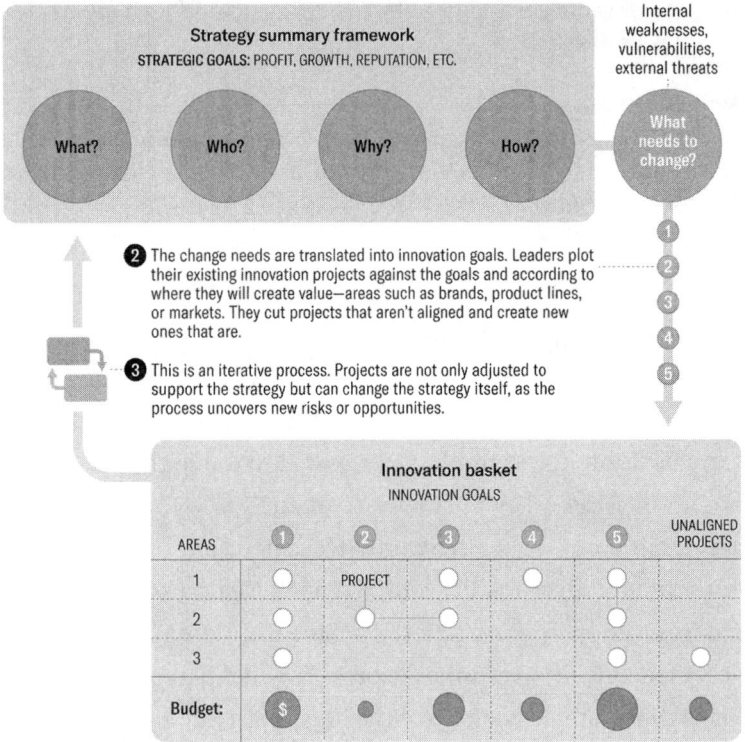

Strategy summary framework
STRATEGIC GOALS: PROFIT, GROWTH, REPUTATION, ETC.

Internal weaknesses, vulnerabilities, external threats

What? Who? Why? How? What needs to change?

2 The change needs are translated into innovation goals. Leaders plot their existing innovation projects against the goals and according to where they will create value—areas such as brands, product lines, or markets. They cut projects that aren't aligned and create new ones that are.

3 This is an iterative process. Projects are not only adjusted to support the strategy but can change the strategy itself, as the process uncovers new risks or opportunities.

Innovation basket
INNOVATION GOALS

AREAS	①	②	③	④	⑤	UNALIGNED PROJECTS
1	○	PROJECT	○	○	○	
2	○	○	○		○	
3	○				○	○
Budget:	$	•	●	●	●	●

way, we differentiate the concept from finance and avoid the mistake of treating projects like financial securities, where the goal is usually to maximize returns through diversification. It's important to remember that innovation projects are creative acts, whereas investment in financial securities is simply the purchase of assets that have already been created.

The top row of the basket lists the change needs from the first exercise, now framed as the innovation goals that projects are expected to address. Examples include reducing manufacturing costs, improving quality, developing new products, creating accelerated or more-flexible sales processes, and introducing an after-sales service process or a sales channel in a new country. The left-hand column identifies where in the unit's business model the project is expected to add value, such as its brands, product lines, or market segments.

Unlike a portfolio, the basket is customized to the business unit's strategy and organization. The goals in the framework are not generic: They directly reflect the company's strategy for the unit—and identify which part of the business model they'll add value to.

Filling the basket

Next, executives locate the company's existing innovation projects in the basket, with the understanding that some may straddle multiple goals and areas. For each project, leaders should ask, "How does this help the unit achieve its strategic innovation goals?" Or, put another way, "How does it address our strategic gaps?" If a project addresses an identified change need, it fits the strategy and belongs in the basket. But in many cases, projects may deliver different changes from those identified as opportunities, or little change at all. Those go into the "unaligned" column. Some projects may deliver a financial benefit that does not translate into sustainable competitive advantage. In those cases, if they are not too advanced they should be dropped.

Once the basket has been winnowed of projects that do not align with strategic goals, it's time to begin adding new ones that are consistent with the strategy. This should not be a top-down deductive process but rather a creative endeavor, carried out in workshops with the management team and relevant experts. It will require substantial contributions of project ideas from frontline staff, who often know a great deal more than management might expect about what adds value to the unit. Designing an innovation basket will launch a creative discussion of what opportunities exist (much as what takes place in a design-thinking workshop) and how they can be translated into a collection of projects that support the unit's competitive strategy.

After the business unit has gone through the basket cycle a couple of times, the alignment won't need to be designed from scratch again. It will evolve with the strategic environment, the strategic position, and the basket's own contents as projects are finished and removed, allowing room for new ones to enter.

Evaluation of the basket may trigger a change of strategy. It may, for example, reveal aspects of the competitive position that were overlooked or new opportunities that could deliver significant value. In such cases the management team needs to revisit the strategy to determine new goals before resuming the basket cycle.

Putting in the numbers

Only after the basket has been filled and reviewed a few times should managers introduce numbers. They can establish targets for each innovation goal (such as reducing unit cost by 10%, launching one new product for each product line, reducing product failures to less than 1% per month, or establishing a functional sales channel in the EU capable of selling

100,000 units within nine months). The basket can then be evaluated by how many of the goals the current slate of projects can deliver on (and, at the end of each year, how much was delivered). With that information, priorities across goals and areas can be established.

It's important not to get to numbers too quickly, because doing so may encourage people to shut down creative options and instead propose only what they can immediately prove. We also caution against letting this part of the process become a formal optimization exercise, in which project selection is driven by an algorithm that precisely weights each project according to its potential for achieving goals. Optimization is inflexible and not transparent and may depend upon standard metrics that do not reflect the dynamics of the environment. Discussion of and commitment to what may seem like a "suboptimal" basket is, after implementation, often superior to what appears on paper to be an "optimal" basket but the story behind which the management team does not fully grasp.

Let's look at how the entire process plays out in practice.

Achieving Focus at Glass, Inc.

We studied the optical devices division of Glass, Inc. (not its real name), a diversified Chinese company. Management felt that growth was suboptimal across the unit's three market segments: telescopes and binoculars, manufacturing optical sensors, and security optical sensors. These three segments became the rows of its innovation basket. The management team embarked on the process we just described in order to identify innovation opportunities within those segments that could deliver its strategic goal of 25% growth per annum.

The team applied the questions of what, who, why, and how to describe the business unit's current strategic position, which is shown in the exhibit "Understanding strategy at Glass, Inc." The exercise identified several strengths and revealed several vulnerabilities—specifically, a cost disadvantage, products whose functionality had become stale, too few new products, relatively weak service in two of three segments, and an aging technology base. (To preserve confidentiality, we aggregated information from the unit's three market segments in the exhibit.)

These weaknesses required strategic changes and became the innovation goals against which the existing innovation basket (projects that were already underway) was evaluated. This exercise revealed that the lion's share of spending was going to new products, which accounted for roughly 80% of the $42 million innovation budget. The other innovation goals were only weakly supported, especially service improvements.

The management team members realized that they had never intended for the unit to have such a strong focus on new products. They diagnosed the cause of the disconnect. Targets for annual revenue growth had compelled management to constantly look for extra revenue, and the path of least resistance had been to develop and introduce incremental product offerings in niche markets. The resulting product proliferation spread resources thin without strengthening competitive advantage. As the unit CEO reflected, their focus on offering a wide swath of products to achieve short-term revenue goals had put them in a weakened competitive position.

Not only did the innovation basket need to change but so did the unit's strategic goals and how it measured progress toward them. The team went back to the drawing board and embarked on a second cycle of discussions around goals and projects.

Understanding strategy at Glass, Inc.

The unit started by asking four questions to clarify strategy and help set innovation goals. The answers to these questions revealed strengths and weaknesses. The weaknesses, or change needs, then became the unit's five innovation goals.

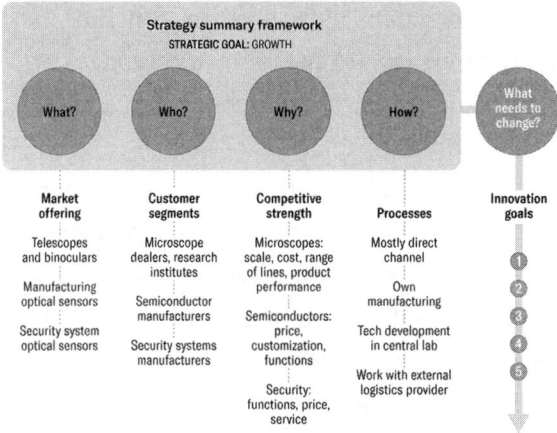

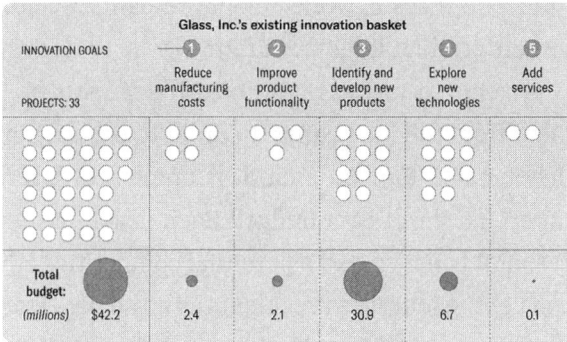

Strategy summary framework
STRATEGIC GOAL: GROWTH

What? — **Who?** — **Why?** — **How?** → **What needs to change?**

Market offering	Customer segments	Competitive strength	Processes	Innovation goals
Telescopes and binoculars	Microscope dealers, research institutes	Microscopes: scale, cost, range of lines, product performance	Mostly direct channel	①
Manufacturing optical sensors	Semiconductor manufacturers	Semiconductors: price, customization, functions	Own manufacturing	②
Security system optical sensors	Security systems manufacturers	Security: functions, price, service	Tech development in central lab	③
			Work with external logistics provider	④
				⑤

Glass, Inc.'s existing innovation basket

INNOVATION GOALS	①	②	③	④	⑤
PROJECTS: 33	Reduce manufacturing costs	Improve product functionality	Identify and develop new products	Explore new technologies	Add services
Total budget: (millions) $42.2	2.4	2.1	30.9	6.7	0.1

When the business unit placed its innovation projects in the basket, it realized that its investments were not aligned with its strategy, prompting the team to stop some projects, create others, and ultimately rebalance its investments.

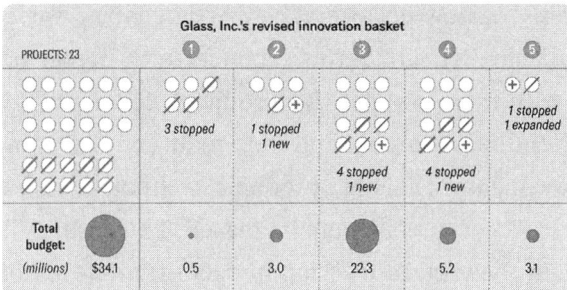

Glass, Inc.'s revised innovation basket

PROJECTS: 23	①	②	③	④	⑤
	3 stopped	1 stopped 1 new	4 stopped 1 new	4 stopped 1 new	1 stopped 1 expanded
Total budget: (millions) $34.1	0.5	3.0	22.3	5.2	3.1

A month later, the innovation basket was markedly different. The unit CEO requested that the group CEO give the unit three years to deliver a strategic change, during which time, instead of relying on the company's standard performance measures, it would track progress toward the innovation goals.

To help the unit get started, we conducted a basket-creation workshop based on the principles of design thinking, and the unit conducted three additional workshops on its own. We asked each participant to write down three innovative ideas that would strengthen the unit's strategic position, which were then discussed, evaluated, and refined in groups of four or five people. Each group presented its three best ideas to the whole workshop, and an idea bank was created.

After much discussion, workshop participants recommended reducing their product lines from four to two, discontinuing 13 of the 33 projects in process, and creating three new projects (two of them from the idea bank). In order to ensure implementation, they created four product-development task forces and gave them each a significant budget. Each task force developed a product that it believed had a potential competitive advantage and had one of the four vice presidents as its chairperson.

The realization that Glass, Inc.'s optical devices division was working on too many unproductive niche products in response to an overly narrow performance metric enabled the group to focus on a smaller number of products with higher potential. Indeed, with more-competitive products, cost-reduction innovations became less urgent and were reduced, while functionality improvements of existing products, technology investments, and service development were increased. This resulted in a 19% decrease in the total innovation budget—from $42.2 million to $34.1 million.

It would be a mistake to conclude from this example that the primary value of the innovation basket is its ability to manage innovation more efficiently, though that may certainly be a bonus in some cases. Engaging with the basket-creation process can lead to a fundamental change in strategy. Let's look at a case in point.

Strategic Reinvention at BAT

When the lead-acid (LA) battery unit of the battery company BAT (not its real name) used our process, it had a transformational impact on both competitive and organizational strategy. BAT saw considerable opportunities in the rise of renewable energy and had created a specialist unit for developing large lithium batteries to store energy produced by wind farms, solar arrays, and other renewable sources. But it still believed there was growth potential for the "old" lead-acid technology in car batteries, and it set an annual growth target of 30% for this market.

The LA battery unit's primary customers were automotive manufacturers (for new batteries) and dealers and repair shops (for after-sales replacement sales). As long as combustion-engine cars continued to be sold, BAT thought, lead-acid batteries would remain profitable. The LA unit had significant strengths: in particular, low-cost and high-quality products, a wide product range, effective service processes, and competitive product features. It also had a relatively large innovation budget for its size; it invested roughly $20 million annually in approximately 40 projects. But generating growth at the targeted level would require winning new customers, which meant developing new products with novel features and premium product performance. The unit needed to identify which projects to double down on.

When we worked with the unit's top managers to apply our basket analysis to its innovation activities, we uncovered a disconnect between what the leaders thought they were doing and what was actually happening. They thought their innovation projects were focusing on new-product development and significant feature upgrades as a means to drive new growth. But in the unit CEO's words: "To our dismay, the innovation basket showed us that we were spending an excessive share of our innovation budget on cost and quality." The team had been drawn to low-risk projects, in part because the company used quantitative (NPV-related) criteria to choose projects. As a result, new proposals had "drifted toward conservativism," the CEO told us.

The unit managers held two rounds of discussions to identify potential LA opportunities from industry trends and analyses of customer demand. They identified just one: developing extremely compact LA batteries with a slightly lower charge capacity, which would marginally reduce the costs of producing traditional cars. This led to an epiphany: Focusing on LA technologies could not generate sufficient growth in the automotive battery market. Even for combustion-engine cars, LA batteries would gradually give way to denser low-voltage lithium batteries. Moreover, electric vehicles used, in addition to their high-voltage power packs, low-voltage auxiliary batteries that required lithium.

The management team decided it was finally time to consider switching technologies and organized a task force to develop new lithium batteries for the low-voltage car accessories network. The unit did not have to develop the technology from scratch; it could build on the power packs in the lithium battery business unit and in collaboration with a university partner, modifying the technology from high to low voltage and building capability in the new technology in the process. From a company perspective, this decision made sense: The existing lithium unit did not have access to carmakers and dealers, and it was easier for the LA unit to adapt the technology to customer needs than for the lithium unit to develop an understanding of the market needs. This represented a major departure from the business unit's original strategy, and it enhanced collaboration across units.

After four months of work, BAT had a significantly changed innovation basket. Cost reductions and quality improvements remained important and were strengthened. However, management's decision to pursue the large growth opportunity in lithium auxiliary batteries resulted in the doubling of the innovation budget to $40.6 million, with a $20 million investment in an R&D project to develop lithium starter batteries in collaboration with an external research institute and the BAT lithium unit.

As this case illustrates, explicitly exploring the links between a company's strategy and its innovation investments can be transformational. The process helped BAT reposition itself to take advantage of strategic changes in its markets, resulting in a major new investment in a project that straddled traditional boundaries.

A Culture Shift

The process we've explained in this article won't always feel comfortable for managers. In the idea-generation workshops and during strategy discussions, people must feel safe to comment outside their area of expertise and to engage their colleagues—even those above them in the hierarchy—in constructive debate. C-suite executives must be willing to be challenged by colleagues. Not all management teams are prepared to do this.

Functional departments, which often enjoy relative auton-
omy if they meet their KPI targets, will also experience a culture shift. For the basket process to fulfill its potential, each
functional unit must be ready to negotiate its priorities more
explicitly with colleagues in other functions. Marketing must
negotiate with R&D, and both with manufacturing and service
groups. The behaviors necessary for such negotiations cannot
simply be mandated; they must be learned.

A more general challenge is that managers tend to favor
decide-then-act processes, a bias that was present at both our
case examples. Once leaders reach a decision and set a progress
goal for employees, they move on and stop paying attention to
what's been decided. But for our process to work, top management cannot do that. Reducing the connection between a company's strategy and its innovation activities to KPIs hamstrings
the organization's ability to respond and change.

It has long been said that action comes not from rational
deliberation but from emotional engagement, and we see this
time and again in our work. The alignment of the change goals
to the strategy that the managers have embraced triggers a sense
of urgency, and the bottom-up creative involvement sparks
enthusiasm and positive energy. Used in this way, our innovation project-alignment process does not merely help decision-
making, it fosters motivation and a readiness to act.

. . .

The examples we've discussed demonstrate how the innovation
basket process not only helps managers implement strategy
but also helps them shape it. It gives them a window into what
their innovation activities are really doing for their strategy. The

generic risk-reward criteria of traditional portfolio approaches are unlikely to generate much insight, and therefore do not stimulate the type of discussion top managers need to have. Ask yourself: Do you really know how well your innovation investments are aligned with your strategy?

Originally published September–October 2023. Reprint R2305J

A Refresher on Discovery-Driven Planning

by Amy Gallo

You're working on a new venture, and you know you've got to create a plan to execute it. So you look at past projects, gather and analyze relevant market data, make predictions about how much revenue you'll be able to generate, decide what resources you'll need, and set milestones to reach your targets. Right?

Not so fast. That process might work for conventional or ongoing business lines, but new ventures, which are less predictable, require a different set of planning and control tools. That's where the discovery-driven planning (DDP) process comes in.

I talked with Rita McGrath, a professor at Columbia Business School, who together with Ian MacMillan, of the University of Pennsylvania's Wharton School, developed this classic methodology for planning innovation. Their goal was to help entrepreneurs and those inside established companies adopt a new approach, "one better suited to high-potential projects whose prospects are uncertain at the start." Discovery-driven planning has since become a staple in business schools' entrepreneurship curricula and a go-to technique for those who manage innovation.

Where Did Discovery-Driven Planning Originate?

As McGrath and MacMillan explained in their 2014 article, "The Origins of Discovery-Driven Planning," the idea started in the mid-1990s while reviewing the projects Rita tracks in her "flops" file—her collection of failed growth projects that had lost their parent company at least $50 million. In an effort to understand those failed innovations (perfume from the company that makes cheap plastic pens and vegetable-flavored Jello are some examples they cite), they saw a few patterns: "Untested assumptions, taken as facts. Linear plans. Too much funding up front. Little opportunity to redirect when new information was found. And, often, senior executives so besotted with the project that they simply refused to take in information that might have called its direction into question," McGrath explains.

In short, too many firms used conventional planning to manage their new ventures. To help managers avoid these huge mistakes, McGrath and MacMillan came up with a disciplined process to systematically uncover, test, and (if necessary) revise the assumptions behind a venture's plan. They called this new approach "discovery-driven planning" and introduced it in their 1995 HBR article of the same name.

Since then, they have taught the concepts to thousands of students and managers. They've also written about it in their book, *Discovery-Driven Growth*, and in McGrath's latest book, *The End of Competitive Advantage*.

Idea in Brief

The Problem

New ventures are less predictable than conventional or ongoing business lines and require a different set of planning and control tools.

The Solution

Discovery-driven planning (DDP) is a disciplined process to systematically uncover, test, and (if necessary) revise the assumptions behind a venture's plan. It offers a lower-risk way to move a product forward in the face of the unknown.

How It Works

The process has five steps:

1. **Define success** by creating a reverse income statement and calculating the profit margin required and the revenues needed to achieve it.

2. **Benchmark your income statement** against competitors and the market to determine how realistic it is.

3. **Define operational requirements** (all the activities required to produce, sell, or deliver the new product or service).

4. **Document assumptions** and make plans to test them.

5. **Plan for key checkpoints** at which you'll decide if assumptions are holding true and whether to invest more time and money.

What Is Discovery-Driven Planning?

It's a technique that any manager can use when developing and launching a new venture. As McGrath and MacMillan explained in their original article, "conventional planning operates on the premise that managers can extrapolate future results from a well-understood and predictable platform of past experience." But new ventures are uncertain from the start. The assumptions you make at the outset aren't likely to hold up as new information emerges, requiring substantial adjustments to the plan along the way. "In today's popular 'lean' terminology, these adjustments are called 'pivots,'" says McGrath.

Discovery-driven planning offers a lower-risk way to move a product forward in the face of "what is unknown, uncertain, and not yet obvious to the competition" so that firms can "learn as much as possible as cheaply as possible" while pursuing new ventures.

Ultimately, discovery-driven planning is a set of disciplines and tools that includes the following five steps.

Step 1: Define success. Before the venture is launched, decide what success will look like in concrete terms. You start by creating a "reverse income statement" for the project (you can see an example in the original HBR article, "Discovery-Driven Planning."). Instead of estimating the venture's revenues and then assuming profits will come, you determine the profit margin required, which should be at least 10%. You then calculate the revenues needed to deliver that profit.

The key here, says McGrath, is to have a "clear frame" for the venture and a "specific profit model." You're trying to answer the question: What would make the venture worthwhile for you (if you're an entrepreneur) or your company? The reverse income statement forces you to articulate what success would look like and "allows you to see if you're getting off track really early."

There are cases where success can't be measured in financial terms. McGrath says you should still articulate success "in terms of things like number of users, size of network, uptake of a new solution, and so on," and link these outcomes to what might drive them. Ask yourself "what would need to be true to achieve the outcomes you are seeking."

Step 2: Benchmark your income statement. The next step is to "figure out how realistic your reverse income statement is," says McGrath. Here you "benchmark the key revenue and cost metrics in your business against the market and against firms offering the most-comparable products." This will help you quickly assess whether you're being realistic.

McGrath recalls the painful experience of working with a big chemical company that wanted to diversify its business. One of the growth vectors they identified was moving into the production of high-end apparel that would be sold in department stores. "They had had some success trademarking material that went into clothing, so they thought they might move up the value chain," she says.

The team had specified what size they anticipated the market would be by year five, a target number spelled out in the spreadsheets at the back of the plan. But what they found after McGrath helped them do some market sizing and benchmarking "should have killed the project immediately," she says. "One out of every six garments sold in the U.S. would have had to be produced by this company." The project leader was reluctant to stop the project since they'd already put $10 million into it. "He basically argued that advantages in rapid product launch cycles and superior materials technology would ensure that it had a competitive advantage, even in light of the clearly daunting challenge in an industry new to the firm."

The company launched the venture, and "after three months of racking up even more losses, they declared it a flop and withdrew from the market," McGrath explains. "The sad thing about this story is that the company could have learned that the business was unrealistic and stopped it long before spending what they did."

Step 3: Define operational requirements. Next, McGrath says, "you have to think very critically about what has to be true" to realize the profit goals. Lay out all the activities required to produce, sell, and deliver the new product or service to customers. How many salespeople do you need? How many calls do they have to make? How many sales do they have to close and in what time period? McGrath and MacMillan call the investments to perform these activities the venture's "allowable costs."

"Mac always liked to ask his students to specify how they were going to get their 'first five sales,' rather than put grandiose projected revenue numbers in their spreadsheets," they write. Once you've determined these costs, you subtract them from the required revenues and see whether the venture will deliver significant returns. McGrath warns that this is a step that people "often gloss over," but it's critical for determining whether your new venture is worth the risk.

Step 4: Document assumptions. This step is an essential difference between conventional and discovery-driven planning; it's also "where a lot of companies go wrong," according to McGrath. With new ventures, leaders often don't see that they are basing decisions on big assumptions—it's a "huge learning disability" for most companies. To avoid falling into this trap, get everyone together who is working on the venture and list all of the assumptions behind your profit, revenue, and allowable costs calculations. In the beginning, stick to a few of the most critical assumptions, such as what customer problem or need your project addresses. As the cost and risk of the project increase, also increase the thoroughness of your plans to test assumptions. Identifying an assumption now that turns out to be false can save you a lot of pain (and money) later on.

Step 5: Plan for key checkpoints. Now it's time to lay out a plan. But don't create a document that covers today through to launch—"plan only as far out as you have knowledge," McGrath says. Identify a series of checkpoints (which she and MacMillan originally called "milestones" but have since renamed) at which you'll determine whether your assumptions are holding true or need to be redefined. These should be points in time right before your company decides to invest more time and money so that you can either stop the project or redirect it based on what you've learned so far. If your assumptions need to be adjusted, update your reverse income statement and operational requirements.

What Common Mistakes Do People Make When Using Discovery-Driven Planning?

Since people have been using the technique for over two decades, I asked Rita about common mistakes she sees.

The first one is the well-intentioned instinct for "acolytes" of the technique to apply it to all sorts of projects or issues. But, she says, it's "not applicable to everything. You can't use one tool to handle all problems. For example, I wouldn't want to build a $2 billion semiconductor plant with DDP," she says. DDP is most relevant to ventures where there is a lot of uncertainty, and you need to make many assumptions and then test and convert learning quickly. At some point with a new venture, once you've proven its viability, it may make sense to switch to a conventional plan.

The second mistake is to go through the five steps listed above and think you're done. Essential to the methodology is the continual updating of your assumptions and checkpoints. It's a living plan that you have to revisit regularly.

McGrath says that managers need to adapt their mindset when using discovery-driven planning. "People are very afraid of being wrong—and you can't blame them," she says. Without the willingness to figure out that you were wrong about some or all of your assumptions, you can undermine the whole process, warns McGrath. "DDP becomes Kabuki theater, where you're just going through the motions." You should be planning to learn rather than planning to show that you're right. That's why she and MacMillan encourage people to be careful with their language. They prefer "assumption," "guess," and "hypothesis," which show that you're still learning, rather than "projection," "target," or "goal," which "suggest that you've learned all that you need to and can move on."

How Has Discovery-Driven Planning Evolved Since Its Inception?

The technique has proved to be "remarkably durable," says McGrath, but she and MacMillan have made several enhancements, which they explained in the 2014 article. First, they integrated the need to take a close look at future competition, both in generating assumptions and in designing checkpoints that "test whether and when brand-new competitors are emerging, thus better anticipating disruption." Second, they now suggest that you create "assumptions about when competitive attacks and erosion of profits will begin, and design checkpoints as indicators that this is happening so that the next advantage stage can be launched at the optimal time." Third, they suggest that companies stop pursuing ventures more quickly when they turn out to be flawed. "Companies should stop throwing good money and resources once it has become obvious that a venture isn't

going anywhere," she explains. Last, they've shortened the dura-
tion of the plan, suggesting that managers shouldn't think past
more than four checkpoints and should ask themselves, "Do we
have enough money to get through the next three checkpoints?"

These last two additions are a result of how things have
changed over the last 20 years. "The velocity today is so much
faster than it was then," says McGrath. Companies need to make
decisions more quickly. This also means that managers can
be less specific in their early estimates. More people are using
ranges instead of precise numbers, and rather than assuming
the exact size of an opportunity, it's sufficient to say that they
know it's "big," but not how big.

Discovery-driven planning may be more relevant now than it
was 20 years ago. After the original idea was published, in 1995, it
was picked up by Steve Blank, and then by Eric Ries, and became
the foundation of the lean-startup movement. "It's really core to
how we think about innovation today," says McGrath. It's easy to
see how DDP has influenced several lean concepts, including the
minimum viable product and rapid prototyping. While McGrath
and MacMillan didn't talk explicitly about either of those concepts, McGrath says they were implicit in the iterative nature of
their technique.

Adapted from hbr.org, February 13, 2017. Reprint H03G05

4

Know Your Customers' "Jobs to Be Done"

by Clayton M. Christensen, Taddy Hall, Karen Dillon, and David S. Duncan

For as long as we can remember, innovation has been a top priority—and a top frustration—for leaders. In a recent McKinsey poll, 84% of global executives reported that innovation was extremely important to their growth strategies, but a staggering 94% were dissatisfied with their organizations' innovation performance. Most people would agree that the vast majority of innovations fall far short of ambitions.

On paper, this makes no sense. Never have businesses known more about their customers. Thanks to the big data revolution, companies now can collect an enormous variety and volume of customer information, at unprecedented speed, and perform

---

Editor's Note: This chapter is adapted from *Competing Against Luck: The Story of Innovation and Customer Choice* and is reprinted with the permission of HarperBusiness.

sophisticated analyses of it. Many firms have established structured, disciplined innovation processes and brought in highly skilled talent to run them. Most firms carefully calculate and mitigate innovations' risks. From the outside, it looks as if companies have mastered a precise, scientific process. But for most of them, innovation is still painfully hit-or-miss.

What has gone so wrong?

The fundamental problem is, most of the masses of customer data companies create is structured to show correlations: *This customer looks like that one*, or *68% of customers say they prefer version A to version B*. While it's exciting to find patterns in the numbers, they don't mean that one thing actually caused another. And though it's no surprise that correlation isn't causality, we suspect that most managers have grown comfortable basing decisions on correlations.

Why is this misguided? Consider the case of one of this article's coauthors, Clayton Christensen. He's 64 years old. He's six feet eight inches tall. His shoe size is 16. He and his wife have sent all their children off to college. He drives a Honda minivan to work. He has a lot of characteristics, but none of them has caused him to go out and buy the *New York Times*. His reasons for buying the paper are much more specific. He might buy it because he needs something to read on a plane or because he's a basketball fan and it's March Madness time. Marketers who collect demographic or psychographic information about him—and look for correlations with other buyer segments—are not going to capture those reasons.

After decades of watching great companies fail, we've come to the conclusion that the focus on correlation—and on knowing more and more about customers—is taking firms in the wrong

Idea in Brief

What's Wrong

Innovation success rates are shockingly low worldwide, and have been for decades.

What's Needed

Marketers and product developers focus too much on customer profiles and on correlations unearthed in data, and not enough on what customers are trying to achieve in a particular circumstance.

What's Effective

Successful innovators identify poorly performed "jobs" in customers' lives—and then design products, experiences, and processes around those jobs.

direction. What they really need to home in on is the progress that the customer is trying to make in a given circumstance—what the customer hopes to accomplish. This is what we've come to call the *job to be done*.

We all have many jobs to be done in our lives. Some are little (pass the time while waiting in line); some are big (find a more fulfilling career). Some surface unpredictably (dress for an out-of-town business meeting after the airline lost my suitcase); some regularly (pack a healthful lunch for my daughter to take to school). When we buy a product, we essentially "hire" it to help us do a job. If it does the job well, the next time we're confronted with the same job, we tend to hire that product again. And if it does a crummy job, we "fire" it and look for an alternative. (We're using the word "product" here as shorthand for any solution that companies can sell; of course, the full set of "candidates" we consider hiring can often go well beyond just offerings from companies.)

This insight emerged over the past two decades in a course taught by Clay at Harvard Business School. (See "Marketing Malpractice," HBR, December 2005.) The theory of jobs to be done was developed in part as a complement to the theory of disruptive innovation—which at its core is about competitive responses to innovation: It explains and predicts the behavior of companies in danger of being disrupted and helps them understand which new entrants pose the greatest threats.

But disruption theory doesn't tell you how to create products and services that customers want to buy. Jobs-to-be-done theory does. It transforms our understanding of customer choice in a way that no amount of data ever could, because it gets at the causal driver behind a purchase.

The Business of Moving Lives

A decade ago, Bob Moesta, an innovation consultant and a friend of ours, was charged with helping bolster sales of new condominiums for a Detroit-area building company. The company had targeted downsizers—retirees looking to move out of the family home and divorced single parents. Its units were priced to appeal to that segment—$120,000 to $200,000—with high-end touches to give a sense of luxury. "Squeakless" floors. Triple-waterproof basements. Granite counters and stainless steel appliances. A well-staffed sales team was available six days a week for any prospective buyer who walked in the door. A generous marketing campaign splashed ads across the relevant Sunday real estate sections.

The units got lots of traffic, but few visits ended up converting to sales. Maybe bay windows would be better? Focus group participants thought that sounded good. So the architect scrambled to add bay windows (and any other details that the focus group suggested) to a few showcase units. Still sales did not improve.

Although the company had done a cost-benefit analysis of all the details in each unit, it actually had very little idea what made the difference between a tire kicker and a serious buyer. It was easy to speculate about reasons for poor sales: bad weather, underperforming salespeople, the looming recession, holiday slowdowns, the condos' location. But instead of examining those factors, Moesta took an unusual approach: He set out to learn from the people who had bought units what job they were hiring the condominiums to do. "I asked people to draw a timeline of how they got here," he recalls. The first thing he learned, piecing together patterns in scores of interviews, was what did *not* explain who was most likely to buy. There wasn't a clear demographic or psychographic profile of the new-home buyers, even though all were downsizers. Nor was there a definitive set of features that buyers valued so much that it tipped their decisions.

But the conversations revealed an unusual clue: the dining room table. Prospective customers repeatedly told the company they wanted a big living room, a large second bedroom for visitors, and a breakfast bar to make entertaining easy and casual; on the other hand, they didn't need a formal dining room. And yet, in Moesta's conversations with actual buyers, the dining room table came up repeatedly. "People kept saying, 'As soon as I figured out what to do with my dining room table, then I was free to move,'" reports Moesta. He and his colleagues couldn't understand why the dining room table was such a big deal. In most cases people were referring to well-used, out-of-date furniture that might best be given to charity—or relegated to the local dump.

But as Moesta sat at his own dining room table with his family over Christmas, he suddenly understood. Every birthday was spent around that table. Every holiday. Homework was spread out on it. The table represented family.

What was stopping buyers from making the decision to move, he hypothesized, was not a feature that the construction company had failed to offer but rather the anxiety that came with giving up something that had profound meaning. The decision to buy a six-figure condo, it turned out, often hinged on a family member's willingness to take custody of a clunky piece of used furniture.

That realization helped Moesta and his team begin to grasp the struggle potential home buyers faced. "I went in thinking we were in the business of new-home construction," he recalls. "But I realized we were in the business of moving lives."

With this understanding of the job to be done, dozens of small but important changes were made to the offering. For example, the architect managed to create space in the units for a dining room table by reducing the size of the second bedroom. The company also focused on easing the anxiety of the move itself: It provided moving services, two years' worth of storage, and a sorting room within the condo development where new owners could take their time making decisions about what to discard.

The insight into the job the customers needed done allowed the company to differentiate its offering in ways competitors weren't likely to copy—or even comprehend. The new perspective changed everything. The company actually raised prices by $3,500, which included (profitably) covering the cost of moving and storage. By 2007, when industry sales were off by 49% and the market was plummeting, the developers had actually grown business by 25%.

Getting a Handle on the Job to Be Done

Successful innovations help consumers to solve problems—to make the progress they need to, while addressing any anxieties or inertia that might be holding them back. But we need to be clear: "Job to be done" is not an all-purpose catchphrase. Jobs are complex and multifaceted; they require precise definition. Here are some principles to keep in mind:

"Job" is shorthand for what an individual really seeks to accomplish in a given circumstance

But this goal usually involves more than just a straightforward task; consider the experience a person is trying to create. What the condo buyers sought was to transition into a new life, in the specific circumstance of downsizing—which is completely different from the circumstance of buying a first home.

The *circumstances* are more important than customer characteristics, product attributes, new technologies, or trends

Before they understood the underlying job, the developers focused on trying to make the condo units ideal. But when they saw innovation through the lens of the customers' circumstances, the competitive playing field looked totally different. For example, the new condos were competing not against other new condos but against the idea of no move at all.

Good innovations solve problems that formerly had only inadequate solutions—or no solution

Prospective condo buyers were looking for simpler lives without the hassles of home ownership. But to get that, they thought, they had to endure the stress of selling their current homes, wading through exhausting choices about what to keep. Or they could stay where they were, even though that solution would become increasingly imperfect as they aged. It was only when given a third option that addressed all the relevant criteria that shoppers became buyers.

Jobs are never simply about function—they have powerful social and emotional dimensions

Creating space in the condo for a dining room table reduced a very real anxiety that prospective buyers had. They could take the table with them if they couldn't find a home for it. And having two years' worth of storage and a sorting room on the premises gave condo buyers permission to work slowly through the emotions involved in deciding what to keep and what to discard. Reducing their stress made a catalytic difference.

These principles are described here in a business-to-consumer context, but jobs are just as important in B2B settings. For an example, see the sidebar "Doing Jobs for B2B Customers."

Designing Offerings Around Jobs

A deep understanding of a job allows you to innovate without guessing what trade-offs your customers are willing to make. It's a kind of job spec.

Of the more than 20,000 new products evaluated in Nielsen's 2012–2016 Breakthrough Innovation report, only 92 had sales of more than $50 million in year one and sustained sales in year two, excluding close-in line extensions. (Coauthor Taddy Hall is the lead author of Nielsen's report.) On the surface the list of hits might seem random—International Delight Iced Coffee, Hershey's Reese's Minis, and Tidy Cats Lightweight, to name just a few—but they have one thing in common. According to Nielsen, every one of them nailed a poorly performed and very specific job to be done. International Delight Iced Coffee let people enjoy in their homes the taste of coffeehouse iced drinks they'd come to love. And thanks to Tidy Cats Lightweight litter, millions of cat owners no longer had to struggle with getting heavy, bulky boxes off store shelves, into car trunks, and up the stairs into their homes.

How did Hershey's achieve a breakout success with what might seem to be just another version of the decades-old peanut butter cup? Its researchers began by exploring the circumstances in which Reese's enthusiasts were "firing" the current product formats. They discovered an array of situations—driving the car, standing in a crowded subway, playing a video game—in which the original large format was too big and messy, while the smaller, individually wrapped cups were a hassle (opening them required two hands). In addition, the accumulation of the cups' foil wrappers created a guilt-inducing tally of consumption: *I had* that *many?* When the company focused on the job that smaller versions of Reese's were being hired to do, it created Reese's Minis. They have no foil wrapping to leave a telltale trail, and they come in a resealable flat-bottom bag that a consumer can easily dip a single hand into. The results were astounding: $235 million in the first two years' sales and the birth of a breakthrough category extension.

Creating customer experiences

Identifying and understanding the job to be done are only the first steps in creating products that customers want—especially ones they will pay premium prices for. It's also essential to create the

Identifying Jobs to Be Done

Jobs analysis doesn't require you to throw out the data and research you've already gathered. Personas, ethnographic research, focus groups, customer panels, competitive analysis, and so on can all be perfectly valid starting points for surfacing important insights. Here are five questions for uncovering jobs your customers need help with.

Do you have a job that needs to be done?

In a data-obsessed world, it might be a surprise that some of the greatest innovators have succeeded with little more than intuition to guide their efforts. Pleasant Rowland saw the opportunity for American Girl dolls when searching for gifts that would help her connect with her nieces. Sheila Marcelo started Care.com, the online "matchmaking" service for child care, senior care, and pet care, after struggling with her family's own care needs. Now, less than 10 years later, it boasts more than 19 million members across 16 countries and revenues approaching $140 million.

Where do you see nonconsumption?

You can learn as much from people who aren't hiring any product as from those who are. Nonconsumption is often where the most fertile opportunities lie, as one university found when it reached out to older learners.

What work-arounds have people invented?

If you see consumers struggling to get something done by cobbling together work-arounds, pay attention. They're probably deeply unhappy with the available solutions—and a promising base of new business. When Intuit noticed that small-business owners were using Quicken—designed for individuals—to do accounting for their firms, it realized small firms represented a major new market.

What tasks do people want to avoid?

There are plenty of jobs in daily life that we'd just as soon get out of. We call these "negative jobs." Harvard Business School alum Rick Krieger and some partners decided to start QuickMedx, the forerunner of CVS MinuteClinics, after Krieger spent a frustrating few hours waiting in an emergency room for his son to get a strep-throat test. MinuteClinics can see walk-in patients instantly, and their nurse practitioners can prescribe medicines for routine ailments, such as conjunctivitis, ear infections, and strep throat.

What surprising uses have customers invented for existing products?

Recently, some of the biggest successes in consumer packaged goods have resulted from a job identified through unusual uses of established products. For example, NyQuil had been sold for decades as a cold remedy, but it turned out that some consumers were knocking back a couple of spoonfuls to help them sleep, even when they weren't sick. Hence, ZzzQuil was born, offering consumers the good night's rest they wanted without the other active ingredients they didn't need.

right set of experiences for the purchase and use of the product and then integrate those experiences into a company's processes.

When a company does that, it's hard for competitors to catch up. Take American Girl dolls. If you don't have a preteen girl in your life, you may not understand how anyone could pay more than a hundred dollars for a doll and shell out hundreds more for clothing, books, and accessories. Yet to date the business has sold 29 million dolls, and it racks up more than $500 million in sales annually.

What's so special about American Girls? Well, it's not the dolls themselves. They come in a variety of styles and ethnicities and are lovely, sturdy dolls. They're *nice,* but they aren't *amazing.* Yet for nearly 30 years they have dominated their market. When you see a product or service that no one has successfully copied, the product itself is rarely the source of the long-term competitive advantage.

American Girl has prevailed for so long because it's not really selling dolls: It's selling an experience. Individual dolls represent different times and places in U.S. history and come with books that relate each doll's backstory. For girls, the dolls provide a rich opportunity to engage their imaginations, connect with friends who also own the dolls, and create unforgettable memories with their mothers and grandmothers. For parents—the buyers—the dolls help engage their daughters in a conversation about the generations of women that came before them—about their struggles, their strength, their values and traditions.

American Girl founder Pleasant Rowland came up with the idea when shopping for Christmas presents for her nieces. She didn't want to give them hypersexualized Barbies or goofy Cabbage Patch Kids aimed at younger children. The dolls—and their worlds—reflect Rowland's nuanced understanding of the job preteen girls hire the dolls to do: help articulate their feelings and validate who they are—their identity, their sense of self, and their cultural and racial background—and make them feel they can surmount the challenges in their lives.

There are dozens of American Girl dolls representing a broad cross section of profiles. Kaya, for example, is a young girl from a Northwest Native American tribe in the late 18th century. Her backstory tells of her leadership, compassion, courage, and loyalty. There's Kirsten Larson, a Swedish immigrant who settles in the Minnesota territory and faces hardships and challenges but triumphs in the end. And so on. A significant part of the allure is the well-written, historically accurate books about each character's life.

Rowland and her team thought through every aspect of the experience required to perform the job. The dolls were never sold in traditional toy stores. They were available only through mail order or at American Girl stores, which were initially located in just a few major metropolitan areas. The stores have doll hospitals that can repair tangled hair or fix broken parts. Some have restaurants in which parents, children, and their dolls can enjoy a kid-friendly menu—or where parents can host birthday parties. A trip to the American Girl store has become a special day out, making the dolls a catalyst for family experiences that will be remembered forever.

No detail was too small to consider. Take the sturdy red-and-pink boxes the dolls come in. Rowland remembers the debate over whether to wrap them with narrow cardboard strips, known as "belly bands." Because the bands each added 2 cents and 27 seconds to the packaging process, the designers suggested skipping them. Rowland says she rejected the idea out of hand: "I said, 'You're not getting it. What has to happen to make this special to the child? I don't want her to see some shrink-wrapped thing coming out of the box. The fact that she has to wait just a split second to get the band off and open the tissue under the lid makes it exciting to open the box. It's not the same as walking down the aisle in the toy store and picking a Barbie off the shelf.'"

In recent years Toys "R" Us, Walmart, and even Disney have all tried to challenge American Girl's success with similar dolls—at a small fraction of the price. Though American Girl, which was acquired by Mattel, has experienced some sales declines in the past two years, to date no competitor has managed to make a dent in its market dominance. Why? Rowland thinks that competitors saw themselves in the "doll business," whereas she never lost sight of why the dolls were cherished: the experiences and stories and connections that they enable.

Aligning processes

The final piece of the puzzle is processes—how the company integrates across functions to support the job to be done. Processes are often hard to see, but they matter profoundly. As MIT's Edgar Schein has discussed, processes are a critical part of an organization's unspoken culture. They tell people inside the company, "This is what matters most to us." Focusing processes on the job to be done provides clear guidance to everyone on the team. It's a simple but powerful way of making sure a company doesn't unintentionally abandon the insights that brought it success in the first place.

A good case in point is Southern New Hampshire University, which has been lauded by *U.S. News & World Report* (and other publications) as one of the most innovative colleges in America. After enjoying a 34% compounded annual growth rate for six years, SNHU was closing in on $535 million in annual revenues at the end of fiscal 2016.

Like many similar academic institutions, SNHU once struggled to find a way to distinguish itself and survive. The university's longtime bread-and-butter strategy had relied on appealing to a traditional student body: 18-year-olds, fresh out of high school, continuing their education. Marketing and outreach were generic, targeting everyone, and so were the policies and delivery models that served the school.

SNHU had an online "distance learning" academic program that was "a sleepy operation on a nondescript corner of the main campus," as president Paul LeBlanc describes it. Yet it had attracted a steady stream of students who wanted to resume an aborted run at a college education. Though the online program was a decade old, it was treated as a side project, and the university put almost no resources into it.

On paper, both traditional and online students might look similar. A 35-year-old and an 18-year-old working toward an accounting degree need the same courses, right? But LeBlanc and his team saw that the job the online students were hiring SNHU to do had almost nothing in common with the job that "coming of age" undergraduates hired the school to do. On average, online students are 30 years old, juggling work and family, and trying to squeeze in an education. Often they still carry debt from an earlier college experience. They're not looking for social activities or a campus scene. They need higher education to provide just four things: convenience, customer service, credentials, and speedy completion times. That, the team realized, presented an enormous opportunity.

SNHU's online program was in competition not with local colleges but with other national online programs, including those offered by both traditional colleges and for-profit schools like the University of Phoenix and ITT Technical Institute. Even more significantly, SNHU was competing with *nothing*. Nonconsumption. Suddenly, the market that had seemed finite and hardly worth fighting for became one with massive untapped potential.

But very few of SNHU's existing policies, structures, and processes were set up to support the actual job that online students needed done. What had to change? "Pretty much everything," LeBlanc recalls. Instead of treating online learning as a second-class citizen, he and his team made it their focus. During a session with about 20 faculty members and administrators, they charted the entire admissions process on a whiteboard. "It

Doing Jobs for B2B Customers

Des Traynor is a cofounder of Intercom, which makes software that helps companies stay in touch with customers via their websites, mobile apps, email, and Facebook Messenger.

Intercom, which now has more than 10,000 customers and grew fourfold in 2015, adopted a jobs-to-be-done perspective to clarify its strategy in 2011, when it was still an early-stage startup. Traynor spoke about that experience with Derek van Bever and Laura Day of Harvard Business School's Forum for Growth & Innovation. Here is an edited version of their conversation.

Forum: *How did you come across the "jobs" approach to innovation and strategy?*

Traynor: Somewhat by accident! In 2011 Intercom had just four engineers and some modest VC backing. I was asked to speak about managing a startup at a conference. Clay Christensen opened the conference and mentioned "jobs to be done."

And that made an impression because ... ?

We were searching for direction at the time. We knew we wanted to help internet companies talk to their customers—and to make that personal. We knew that the features we shipped were valuable—but we didn't really know who was using us. Customer support? Marketing? Market research? Nor did we know exactly what they were using us for.

How had you approached those questions until then?

We were using a personas-based approach to segmentation, but it wasn't working. We had too many "typical users" who had little in common, going by traits like demographics or job titles. Because we didn't really understand why people were coming to the platform—what they were using it for—we charged a single price for access to the entire platform.

As soon as I grasped the distinction between "customers" and "problems people need help with," a light bulb went off. I called my cofounder Eoghan McCabe and said, "We're going to build a company that is focused on doing a job."

And how did you figure out what the relevant job was?

We got in touch with innovation consultant Bob Moesta, who has a lot of practical experience with this approach. Bob and his team conducted individual interviews with two types of customers: people who had recently signed on with us, and people who had dropped the service or changed their usage significantly.

He wanted to understand the timeline of events that led up to a purchasing decision and the "forces" that ultimately pushed people into that decision. Bob has a theory that customers always experience conflict when considering a new purchase—what he calls "the struggling moment." There are pressures pushing them to act—to solve a problem by "hiring" a solution—and forces like inertia, fear of change, and anxiety holding them back. His overall objective was to explain, in the customers' words, what caused people to resolve the conflict and "hire" Intercom, and then how well Intercom performed.

I listened in on four interviews live—and tried not to jump to judgment. Two things stood out. One, prospective clients who sampled our services were usually flailing. Their growth had flattened, and they were ready to try something new. And two, the words they described our product with were really different from the words we used. People using it to sign up new customers kept using the word "engage," for example. We used the term "outbound messaging," which has a very different feel.

According to Bob, this is really common: Companies fall in love with their own jargon. They focus on the technology being offered rather than the value being delivered.

What did you learn about the jobs you were being hired to do?

It turned out that people had four distinct jobs: First, help me observe. Show me the people who use my product and what they do with it. Second, help me engage—to convert sign-ups into active users. Third, help me learn—give me rich feedback from the right people. And finally, help me support—to fix my customers' problems.

(*continued*)

Doing Jobs for B2B Customers (*continued*)

How much did you change the business once you understood the different jobs your customers had?

A lot. We now offer four distinct services, each designed to support one of those jobs. Our R&D group—120 people—has four teams, one for each job, and we've gone deeper and deeper on each job.

Essentially, we realized that we'd been offering a one-size-fits-none service. The initial price felt high because no customer needed everything we were selling.

How did that change work out?

Our conversion rate has increased, since prospects can now buy just the piece of the site that suits their initial job, and we're able to establish multiple points of sale across client organizations, since there is now a logical path for relationship growth.

looked like a schematic from a nuclear submarine!" he says. The team members circled all the hurdles that SNHU was throwing up—or not helping people overcome—in that process. And then, one by one, they eliminated those hurdles and replaced them with experiences that would satisfy the job that online students needed to get done. Dozens of decisions came out of this new focus.

Here are some key questions the team worked through as it redesigned SNHU's processes:

What experiences will help customers make the progress they're seeking in a given circumstance?

For older students, information about financial aid is critical; they need to find out if continuing their education is even possible, and time is of the essence. Often they're researching options late at night, after a long day, when the kids have finally gone to sleep. So responding to a prospective student's inquiry with a generic email 24 hours later would often miss the window of opportunity. Understanding the context, SNHU set an internal goal of a follow-up phone call within eight and a half minutes. The swift personal response makes prospective students much more likely to choose SNHU.

What obstacles must be removed?

Decisions about a prospect's financial aid package and how much previous college courses would count toward an SNHU degree were resolved within days instead of weeks or months.

What are the social, emotional, and functional dimensions of the job?

Ads for the online program were completely reoriented toward later-life learners. They attempted to resonate not just with the functional dimensions of the job, such as getting the training needed to advance in a career, but also with the emotional and social ones, such as the pride people feel in earning their degrees. One ad featured an SNHU bus roaming the country handing out large framed diplomas to online students who couldn't be on campus for graduation. "Who did you get this degree for?" the voice-over asks, as the commercial captures glowing graduates in their homes. "I got it for me," one woman says, hugging her diploma. "I did this for my mom," beams a 30-something man. "I did it for you, bud," one father says, holding back tears as his young son chirps, "Congratulations, Daddy!"

But perhaps most important, SNHU realized that enrolling prospects in their first class was only the beginning of doing the job. The school sets up each new online student with a personal adviser, who stays in constant contact—and notices red flags even before the students might. This support is far more critical to continuing education students than traditional ones, because so many obstacles in their everyday lives conspire against them. Haven't checked out this week's assignment by Wednesday or Thursday? Your adviser will touch base with you. The unit test went badly? You can count on a call from your adviser to see not only what's going on with the class but what's going on in your life. Your laptop is causing you problems? An adviser might just send you a new one. This unusual level of assistance is a key reason that SNHU's online programs have extremely high Net Promoter Scores (9.6 out of 10) and a graduation rate—about 50%—topping that of virtually every community college (and far above that of costlier, for-profit rivals, which have come under fire for low graduation rates).

SNHU has been open with would-be competitors, offering tours and visits to executives from other educational institutions. But the experiences and processes the university has created for online students would be difficult to copy. SNHU did not invent all its tactics. But what it has done, with laser focus, is ensure that its hundreds and hundreds of processes are tailored to the job students are hiring the school for.

. . .

Many organizations have unwittingly designed innovation processes that produce inconsistent and disappointing outcomes. They spend time and money compiling data-rich models that make them masters of description but failures at prediction. But firms don't have to continue down that path. Innovation can be far more predictable—and far more profitable—if you start by identifying jobs that customers are struggling to get done. Without that lens, you're doomed to hit-or-miss innovation. With it, you can leave relying on luck to your competitors.

Originally published in September 2016. Reprint R1609D

5

Breaking Down the Barriers to Innovation

by Scott D. Anthony, Paul Cobban, Rahul Nair, and Natalie Painchaud

To catalyze innovation, companies have invested billions in internal venture capital, incubators, accelerators, and field trips to Silicon Valley. Yet according to a McKinsey survey, 94% of executives are dissatisfied with their firms' innovation performance. Across industries, one survey after another has found the same thing: Businesses just aren't getting the impact they want, despite all their spending. Why? We believe that it's because they've failed to address a huge underlying obstacle: the day-to-day routines and rituals that stifle innovation.

Fortunately, it's possible to "hack" this problem. Drawing on the behavioral-change literature and on our experiences working with dozens of global companies, including DBS, Southeast Asia's biggest bank, we've devised a practical way to break bad habits that squelch innovation and to develop new ones that inspire it.

Like most hacks, our approach isn't expensive, though it does take time and energy. It involves setting up interventions we call BEANs, shorthand for *behavior enablers, artifacts,* and *nudges.* Behavior enablers are tools or processes that make it easier for people to do something different. Artifacts—things you can see and touch—support the new behavior. And nudges, a tactic drawn from behavioral science, promote change through indirect suggestion and reinforcement. Though the acronym may sound a bit glib, we've found that it's simple and memorable in a way that's useful for organizations trying to develop better habits.

In this article we'll describe a variety of BEANs that firms have used to unleash innovation, the characteristics that make them effective, and how your organization can develop and implement its own BEANs. But first we'll briefly examine the behaviors that drive innovation and the barriers that thwart it.

Innovation Behaviors and Blockers

To us, innovation doesn't mean mere inventiveness. In our work we define it as "something different that creates value." It isn't just the purview of engineers and scientists, nor is it limited to new-product development. Processes can be innovated. Marketing approaches can too. Something different can be a big breakthrough, but it can also be an everyday improvement that makes the complicated a bit simpler or the expensive more affordable.

In our work and research, we've found that the most innovative organizations exhibit five key behaviors: They always assume there's a better way to do things. They focus on deeply understanding customers' stated and unstated needs and desires. They collaborate across and beyond the organization,

Idea in Brief

The Challenge

Companies' investments in innovation are stymied by the day-to-day routines and habits that stifle original thinking.

The Solution

Leadership needs to identify these innovation blockers and neutralize them with interventions called "BEANs"—behavior enablers, artifacts, and nudges.

The Outcome

The bank DBS used this approach to unleash innovation at a tech-development center. Engagement scores rose 20%, and the center was named a great place to innovate.

actively cross-pollinating. They recognize that success requires experimentation, rapid iteration, and frequent failure. Last, they empower people to take considered risks, voice dissenting opinions, and seek needed resources.

None of those behaviors is surprising. It's just puzzling that they aren't more common. After all, as children, most of us were creative, curious, collaborative, and risk-taking. But once we went to school and, later, to work, those behaviors got quashed. Students and employees are taught there's a right way to do things. That raising questions and expressing dissent, even benignly, is risky. As people learn those rules, the innovation muscles that were toned in their youth atrophy. That may explain why kindergarten graduates generally outperform new MBAs on "the marshmallow challenge," a timed competition to use spaghetti, tape, and string to build the tallest structure that will support a marshmallow on top.

Ask executives what stands in the way of innovation, and they'll point to real barriers, such as a lack of time (few executives or organizations have slack capacity to spend on new thinking); the perception that doing things differently produces no benefits, just costs (and possibly punishment); a lack of innovation skills; and a lack of infrastructure for bringing ideas to fruition. But one of the biggest impediments is organizational inertia. As an executive once said to us, businesses are "organized to deliver predictable, reliable results—and that's exactly the problem." A major paradox managers face is that the systems that enable success with today's model reinforce behaviors that are inconsistent with discovering tomorrow's model.

If you don't address inertia, efforts to eliminate other blockers won't work. Give people more time in an environment stifled by inertia, and they'll simply have more time to do things the old way; give them new skills, and those will go to waste if they don't fit with existing routines. Fortunately, you can combat both inertia and other blockers with BEANs. Now let's look at an initiative that did just that.

Breaking Down Innovation Barriers at DBS

When Piyush Gupta took over as CEO of DBS, in 2009, he began a multipronged effort to transform it from a stodgy, regulated bank into an agile technology company—or, as he put it, "a 27,000-person startup." Once mocked locally as "Damn Bloody Slow" (for its notoriously long lines), DBS is now considered a global digital leader in financial services, and in 2019 it became the first bank to simultaneously hold the titles "Bank of the Year" (*The Banker*), "Best Bank in the World" (*Global Finance*), and "World's Best Bank" (*Euromoney*).

But back in 2016, DBS was still on its journey. When its top leaders gathered in Singapore to talk about how the bank was progressing, all agreed that though it had made headway, much work remained. In their discussion they identified dysfunctional meetings as a major blocker that entrenched organizational inertia and hindered innovation. Most meetings at DBS could charitably be described as inefficient. They would often start and run late, eating up time that leaders could otherwise have spent on innovation. Sometimes decisions were made, and sometimes they were not. People would dutifully arrive at meetings without a clear sense of why they were there. Some participants were active, but many sat in defensive silence. It's this last point that's most salient. Meetings, leadership concluded, were suppressing diverse voices and reinforcing the status quo.

To change that, DBS introduced a BEAN it called MOJO. It was informed by research at Google that showed that equal share of voice and psychological safety were critical to high-performing, highly innovative project teams. MOJO promotes efficient, effective, open, and collaborative meetings. The MO is the meeting owner, who's responsible for ensuring that the meeting has a clear agenda, that it starts and ends on time, and that all attendees are given an equal say. The JO—or joyful observer—is assigned to help the meeting run crisply and to encourage broad participation. The JO, for example, has the authority to call a "phone Jenga" that requires all attendees to put their phones in a pile on the table. Perhaps most important, at the meeting's end, the JO holds the MO accountable, providing frank feedback about how things went and how the MO can improve. Even when the JO is junior, they are explicitly authorized to be direct with the MO. The presence of an observer and the knowledge that feedback is coming nudge the MO to be mindful of meeting behavior.

This approach, supported by physical reminders in meeting rooms (small cards, wall art, and fun paper cubes that can be tossed around) and a range of measurement and tracking tools, has had a powerful impact. Meetings at DBS no longer run late, saving an estimated 500,000 employee hours to date. Meeting effectiveness, as gauged by ongoing employee surveys, has doubled, and the percentage of employees who say they have an equal share of voice in meetings has jumped from 40% to 90%. Improved efficiency and effectiveness doesn't mean meetings have become dull, however. Living up to their moniker (which reinforces a broader effort at DBS to "make banking joyful"), JOs have even been known to give their feedback in verse. And legends have spread. At one meeting the observer bravely told a senior executive who had lost his cool that the blowup had shut down all discussion. The executive welcomed the feedback, promising to do better next time. It's a story that still circulates, reinforcing the behavioral change DBS hoped to drive with MOJO.

The Keys to Effective BEANs

Over the decades a lot of research has examined why it's so hard for people to break bad habits. Recently, popular books exploring the problem—such as *Switch,* by Chip and Dan Heath; *Nudge,* by Richard Thaler and Cass Sunstein; *The Power of Habit,* by Charles Duhigg; and *Thinking, Fast and Slow,* by Daniel Kahneman—have offered readers a range of practical tools to help. In developing the BEANs solution, we've built on the insights of those academics and practitioners, who've consistently found that it's critical to engage both people's rational, logical side and their emotional, intuitive side. We also drew ideas from long-standing programs like Alcoholics Anonymous and Weight Watchers, which use a combination of mantras, nudges, and social interactions to change people's patterns, and from the science of motivation, which describes how goal setting, achievement, and social comparison and encouragement reinforce desired behaviors.

In our own research we collected some 130 examples of interventions that promoted better innovation habits, which we found either at clients we were working with or by reading through case studies from the Innovation Leader information service and corporate cultural documents compiled by Tettra, a Boston-area startup. Then we and a team from Innosight analyzed those interventions and tested them at a variety of organizations. We determined that successful BEANs typically are:

Simple

Interventions that are easy to adopt and remember gain traction much more quickly.

Fun

When an activity is engaging and social, it's intrinsically rewarding, which makes people more likely to do it—something the science of motivation has long recognized.

Trackable

The ability to monitor performance and compare it against that of others is a powerful motivator. (This is why activity trackers like Fitbit have helped many develop better exercise habits.) So it's critical for BEANs to include a mechanism for measuring their results.

Practical

The best BEANs are smoothly integrated into existing meetings and processes and don't require major changes or entirely new routines.

Reinforced

People often need physical and digital reminders to keep using the new habits.

Organizationally consistent

One of the most cited papers in the change literature is Steven Kerr's 1995 classic "On the Folly of Rewarding A, While Hoping for B." Effective BEANs don't encourage people to do one thing if the company punishes them for that behavior or rewards them for something else.

You can see how all these characteristics come together in MOJO. Another example of a well-crafted BEAN from DBS is the Gandalf scholarship. While Gandalf is the wizard in J.R.R. Tolkien's Lord of the Rings series, the scholarship's name also references DBS's aspiration to be compared to the digital technology giants Google, Apple, Netflix, Amazon, LinkedIn, and Facebook; plop DBS between Netflix and Amazon and you get the acronym. Any employee can apply to receive S$1,000 (about US$740) to spend on a project of their choice—a course, books, a conference—that supports DBS's goal of becoming a learning organization that constantly questions the status quo. The only condition is that winners must teach what they've discovered to their colleagues. As of the fall of 2019, the bank had granted more than 100 scholarships in areas from artificial intelligence to storytelling for managers, with the average recipient teaching close to an additional 300 people. DBS has recorded many of these "teach-backs" and posted them on an online channel with related articles and other information, creating virtual artifacts that have been viewed more than 10,000 times. The bank estimates that each dollar it spends on the scholarships has a positive impact on 30 times as many employees as a dollar spent on traditional training does.

Another good example of a BEAN comes from the Tata Group, India's largest conglomerate. Every year the company holds a celebration honoring innovation accomplishments across its sprawling collection of business units, which range from tea to IT consulting to automobiles. One of the most coveted awards given at that gathering is called Dare to Try. As the name connotes, it goes to a team that failed but in an intelligent way. In the company's words, "Showcasing a growing culture of risk-taking and perseverance across Tata companies . . . [Dare to Try] recognizes and rewards novel, daring and seriously attempted ideas that did not achieve the desired results." Dare to Try is a substantial program, attracting hundreds of applications annually. Promotions for it help nudge innovative behaviors like embracing risk and tolerating failure. The award itself—a trophy—and the high-visibility public summary of the event are artifacts that effectively reinforce Tata's innovation culture.

How to Build a BEAN

While many BEANs, such as MOJO, have sprung up organically, we've created a three-step process companies can use to develop them. We've tested and refined this process through repeated application at DBS and other organizations in a range of industries.

Several of the tests took place at a technology development center in Hyderabad, India, that DBS had set up as part of its digital transformation. The new center was taking over previously outsourced operations such as the design and support of customer-facing mobile applications, and it presented the

Getting Granular About Innovation Behaviors

Too frequently, executives say they want to boost innovation but aren't specific about what that means. Organizations need to get precise about the behaviors they'd like to see. A good approach is to have employees in focus groups on innovation supply endings to the question "Wouldn't it be great if we . . ." Below are examples of various kinds of suggestions that have been generated in such brainstorming sessions:

Questioning the Status Quo

- Were perpetually paranoid about the future?
- Kept an open mind, constantly asking "What if?"
- Avoided shutting down new ideas by saying "This is the way we do things here"?
- Adopted a problem-solver, versus a fault-finder, mindset?

Focusing Intensely on Customers

- Spent more time with customers to understand their jobs to be done?
- Regularly created customer profiles and customer journeys?
- Ensured all solutions were rooted in addressing key customer needs and problems?
- Had deep insight into how customers made decisions between different solutions?

company with the opportunity to build a more entrepreneurial culture from scratch.

The center's office design mimicked what you'd see at any hot young tech venture, with open space, foosball tables, snack bars, and the like. Its recruitment processes, borrowed from

Collaborating Better

- Built cross-functional teams with expertise and viewpoints from different parts of the organization?

- Emphasized collective, versus individual, goals?

- Were transparent and frank while remaining respectful?

- Provided visibility and transparency on initiatives?

Experimenting

- Planned for different scenarios and alternative outcomes?

- Constantly asked ourselves, "What don't we know?" and "How can we learn more?"

- Designed experiments to learn more about key assumptions?

- Rewarded teams for intelligent failure?

Empowering

- Trusted more junior employees to carry out tasks without having to get approval?

- Looked for ways people can bring ideas forward or speak up when something isn't working?

- Owned the outcomes of our decisions without shirking responsibility or playing the blame game?

- Set teams up for success by removing obstacles and providing resources and support?

innovative companies like Netflix, were designed to attract distinctive talent. But when the lights went on, it quickly became clear that employees' day-to-day experiences there had little of that startup feeling. The engineers fell into well-worn routines, working methodically and avoiding fast-paced experimentation.

While employee engagement scores weren't terrible, they were notably short of DBS's aspiration.

To turn things around, a group of Innosight consultants and DBS Technology & Operations change agents (which we'll call the culture team) decided to develop BEANs that would disrupt the unwanted habits and promote new and better ones.

Step 1: Specify the desired characteristics

First the team outlined what kind of organizational traits it wanted, describing a culture that would be agile, learning-oriented, customer-obsessed, data-driven, and experimental. It then listed behaviors under each of them. For example, under "experimental" were aspirational statements such as "We rapidly test new ideas," "We believe in lean experimentation," and "We fail cheap, we fail fast, and we learn even faster."

Step 2: Identify blockers

Next the team looked for things that were getting in the way of the innovative behaviors. To uncover these, members sat in on staff meetings, conducted diagnostic surveys, interviewed center employees one-on-one in confidence, and reviewed "day in the life" journals that developers kept for a week.

Among other issues, the team found that many employees felt they lacked context for their work—an understanding of how their project fit with the broader strategy and what was expected of each person working on the project and of the project overall. Some employees also felt that surfacing problems was taboo, and so they stewed in silent frustration. And some simply felt stretched so thin in their day-to-day work that they lacked time to experiment.

Note that the team was very precise in describing the behaviors it was seeking and their blockers. This is critical; if you don't do this when developing BEANs, you may end up with ersatz blockers or laundry lists that are difficult to tackle. A simple way to identify specific changes you'd like to see is to gather groups of employees and ask them to complete two sentences: "Wouldn't it be great if we . . ." (which surfaces the behaviors; see the sidebar "Getting Granular About Innovation Behaviors") and "But we don't because . . ." (which helps pinpoint the blockers).

Step 3: Come up with interventions

Last the culture team designed ways to eliminate the blockers. To get things going, it facilitated a pair of two-day workshops with senior leaders, one in Hyderabad and the other in Singapore. After discussing the desired behaviors and their blockers, participants broke into small groups for structured brainstorming. Each group was given examples of BEANs from other organizations for inspiration (see the sidebar "BEANs Across Businesses") and, to devise new ones, used a simple template that had the group specify the behaviors sought, the habits blocking them, and the enablers and nudges that would help employees break through them. All the participants then reassembled to review 15 proposed BEANs and vote on a few to implement.

Here are three interventions that were created to tackle lack of context, voice, and time at the center:

Lack of context

This blocker reinforced employees' sense that their business-as-usual approach was good enough. The BEAN targeting it was a "culture canvas" inspired by Alexander Osterwalder and Yves

BEANs Across Businesses

We've identified more than 100 examples of behavior enablers, artifacts, and nudges at work within organizations across industries. While they're all very different, they all serve the purpose of breaking undesirable organizational habits and encouraging new ones. Here are some of our favorites.

Offer a Kickbox

Organization: Adobe

Goal: Encourage experimentation and simplify innovation

Description: Employees apply to receive a red "kickbox" that contains do-it-yourself innovation training, including exercises to perform and a checklist for developing a new product or service idea and pitching it to management. It also contains a prepaid $1,000 debit card to use in validating the concept.

Create a Fail Wall

Organization: Spotify

Goal: Eliminate fear of failure and learn from mistakes

Description: The "fail wall"—a whiteboard with Post-its that publicly celebrates project failures—serves as the starting point for engineering-team postmortems that examine what has been learned and how to prevent similar failures in the future.

Conduct a Premortem

Organization: Atlassian

Goal: Identify threats to new initiatives and develop a defense against them

Description: Before starting a project, teams meet to discuss how it could fail, doing a seven-step exercise that includes a structured cross-examination (in which a group arguing the "success" case questions a group arguing the "failure" case and vice versa), voting to gauge risk severity, assigning risk "owners," and planning how to minimize threats.

Play Lunch Roulette

Organization: Boehringer Ingelheim

Goal: Encourage collaboration and cross-pollination

Description: Lunch roulette is a company website that randomly pairs employees for meals. Participants select a date and a location, click a "match me" button, and simply show up with open minds and a willingness to network.

Go Live from Day One

Organization: Airbnb

Goal: Empower employees with a sense of purpose and responsibility

Description: During the first day of Airbnb's orientation boot camp, engineers are encouraged to push code directly to the website.

Use Games to Develop Leaders

Organization: Tasty Catering

Goal: Help employees think and act like owners

Description: Associates, all of whom are given full visibility into the organization's financials, play a weekly game in which each makes a forecast for a line in the P&L. The projections are then compared with the actual figures. Winners are celebrated and deviations are analyzed, feeding into efforts to identify patterns and generate ideas for further boosting performance.

Pigneur's canvas that maps out the key elements of a business model. The culture canvas is likewise a simple one-page, poster-size template. On it, project teams articulate their business goals and codify team roles and norms. Filling it out helps them gain a clearer sense of expectations, organizational context, and who does what. Giving teams clarity about their goals and the scope to push boundaries further empowers their entrepreneurial spirit. The resulting physical artifact, which includes photos and signatures of members, serves as a visual reminder of teams' commitments.

Lack of voice

A BEAN called "team temp" was devised to liberate employees to speak up when they saw problems. The web-based app, to be used at the first meeting of the week, gauges a project team's mood by inviting members to anonymously enter a score from 1 (highly negative) to 10 (highly positive) and pick a word to describe how they're feeling. This quickly reveals if the team has an issue (a string of 1s and 2s is pretty telling) and prompts a discussion— led by the team leader—about what's going on and how it can be addressed. Because the app tracks team sentiment over time, it also gauges whether interventions are working.

Lack of time

To bust this blocker, the culture team created the "70:20:10" BEAN. Inspired by Google's practices, it gives software developers explicit permission to spend 70% of their time on day-to-day work, 20% on work-improvement ideas, and 10% on experiments and pet projects. By formally freeing up chunks of time for unspecified experimentation, 70:20:10 encourages innovative thinking. To reinforce it, the culture team also created a ritual in which developers shared the learnings of their experimental projects with one another.

These and the other BEANs selected were initially tested by pilot teams in Hyderabad. Their impact was carefully measured, improvements were made, ineffective BEANs were discarded, and effective ones were rolled out more broadly and tracked.

As a result of the 70:20:10 BEAN, for example, teams automated several manual processes, shaving man-hours off key tasks, and developed other innovations. (The initial version of an app to track and improve MOJO results came out of one developer's time for experimentation.) Meanwhile, leaders increased the amount of time they spent walking the halls and modeling the new ways of working.

A year after the interventions began, employee surveys showed that workers' engagement scores at Hyderabad were up 20% and that customer-centricity had risen significantly. In 2018 LinkedIn named the development center one of the top 25 places to work in India, and in 2019 it won a prestigious Zinnov Award as "a great place to innovate."

From "Innoganda" to Impact

Though the DBS story started with a call to action from its CEO, the work in Hyderabad operated several rungs lower in the organization. Indeed, one of the powerful things about BEANs is that they can be effective at the level of a team, a department, or a business unit, or company-wide.

A few words of caution before our parting advice: Companies seeking to spark innovation often copy artifacts they see in other innovative companies. Maybe they install a well-stocked cafeteria with bright colors or provide scooters. But quick-and-easy artifacts that are bolted on and don't connect with day-to-day behaviors won't work.

One of us, Scott, observed an instance of this when he visited a socially oriented venture in Cambodia. It employs thousands of poor artisans, who create garments, carvings, statues, and more. One silkworm farm connected to the venture had put out a bright-blue box and invited workers to leave in it feedback and ideas "for you, for your colleagues, and for your well-being." Sounds inspirational, right?

There was just one problem. The rusted lock on the box betrayed that it hadn't been opened recently—or maybe ever. Such "innoganda"—innovation propaganda—just serves as a painful reminder of the things leadership is not doing. While it may generate a burst of energy at first, it will surely lead to cynicism over the long term.

Even the best BEAN can turn into innoganda without the right support—without (at the risk of torturing the metaphor) someone to tend the soil. When DBS began its journey, many employees, especially leaders, believed that innovation was the preserve of scientific and creative types. To counter that, a DBS team tasked with encouraging cultural change launched programs to teach employees how to innovate. For example, the team partnered with HR to create weeklong events in which executives got three days of training on digital concepts and then took part in a 48-hour "hackathon," joining people from real startups to create prototypes for apps solving real business problems. On the final afternoon the prototypes were pitched to the CEO.

Having executives experience the new mindset and behaviors the company wanted to promote helped make the programs it implemented practical, authentic, and organizationally consistent. Now, when DBS launches new BEANs, they're met not with eye rolls (or, worse, active resistance) but with game curiosity. As BEANs have taken root and proved their value in ways that directly benefit employees and the organization, they've been embraced.

If more and more companies methodically dismantle blockers to innovation and encourage employees to experiment, perhaps we will finally see the gap close between leaders' innovation goals and reality. Remember, when the people in your organization were children, they were brimming with curiosity and creativity. Your job is to bring that youthful spirit back to life.

Originally published in November–December 2019. Reprint R1906E

The Inescapable Paradox of Managing Creativity

by Linda A. Hill, Greg Brandeau, Emily Truelove, and Kent Lineback

When facing the challenge of unleashing organizational innovation, many leaders fail. Some attempt to help their teams flourish by granting almost unlimited freedoms, only to discover that they have created chaos, not high performance. Others try to force their employees' creativity through prescribed programs and activities, which usually yields humdrum results at best.

After studying masters proven at fostering organizational innovation for over 10 years, we have identified the heart of the difficulty. At the core of leading innovation lies a fundamental tension, or paradox, inherent in the leader role: Leaders need to *unleash* individuals' talents yet also *harness* all those diverse talents to yield a useful and cohesive result. On the face of it, this may seem implausible or even impossible, yet evidence supports that both elements are essential. Ideas and possibilities emerge through "unleashing," while "harnessing" aims to ensure that everyone's collective efforts produce a workable solution. To succeed requires the ability to manage the tension between these disparate modes by learning when each is appropriate and by combining them in a never-ending oscillation. Bill Coughran, when he was SVP of engineering with the Infrastructure Group at Google, described this eloquently when he said:

> *Managing tensions in the organization is an ongoing issue . . . you don't want an organization that just salutes and does what you say. You want an organization that argues with you. And so you want to nurture the bottoms-up, but you've got to be careful you don't just degenerate into chaos.*

Six paradoxes of leading innovation

Continually ask yourself where on the continuum your organization falls, and what adjustments should be made.

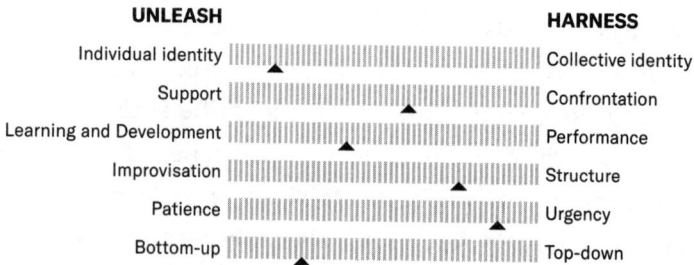

UNLEASH		HARNESS
Individual identity		Collective identity
Support		Confrontation
Learning and Development		Performance
Improvisation		Structure
Patience		Urgency
Bottom-up		Top-down

Idea in Brief

The Problem

Many leaders fail at unleashing innovation in their organizations. Either they create chaos by granting too much freedom, or they produce lack-luster results trying to force creativity through prescribed programs and activities.

Why It's Hard

Over 10 years of research, the authors discovered a fundamental tension at the heart of leading innovation: You must *unleash* individuals' talents to generate ideas yet also *harness* everyone's collective efforts to yield a workable solution.

The Solution

To succeed requires the ability to manage this tension by learning when each mode is appropriate and by combining them in a never-ending oscillation in response to current circumstances.

Our definition of innovation—creating something new and useful—also reflects this paradox. It's easy to think of many new ideas, but it's much more difficult to convert those ideas into something new that actually solves a problem.

To better understand this central paradox of unleashing and harnessing, and its implications for leading innovation, we've broken it down into six constituent paradoxes that almost anyone in an organization will recognize, illustrated in the figure "Six paradoxes of leading innovation.":

Of course, this figure is just a sample—individual leadership styles and organizational needs will vary. When leading innovation, your challenge is to help your organization move appropriately, depending on context and shifting priorities, between unleashing and harnessing on each of these six scales in a process of continuous recalibration. As a leader, you must constantly ask yourself: How will I:

- Affirm each person's need for individual recognition and identity *yet also* tend to the needs of the collective?

- Encourage team members to support one another *while simultaneously* challenging and provoking one another through robust debate?

- Foster experimentation, continuous learning, *and* high performance?

- Determine how much structure—rules, hierarchy, planning, and the like—provides sufficient constraints *without* stifling improvisation?

- Mix patience *and* a sense of urgency?

- Balance bottom-up initiatives *and* top-down interventions?

The "right" position at any moment will depend on specific current circumstances. The goal will always be to take whatever positions enable the collaboration, experimentation, and integration necessary for innovation. Leaders who are on the Harness side will never fully unleash the "slices of genius" in their people (as we called them in our book *Collective Genius*). Those who always stay on the Unleash side will have constant chaos and never solve any problems for the collective good.

This kind of leadership is not easy, especially for leaders who hold conventional notions of top-down leadership, or who find conflict or loss of control uncomfortable. Even skilled leaders of innovation find it hard not to favor one side of the paradox scale over the other. The task of creating new and useful things requires leaders to continually recalibrate the needs of their organizations and to modify their behavior accordingly. They must develop the capacity to lead from the right place on each scale for the moment and situation.

Moreover, real innovation is inherently difficult because the process is so messy and full of the tensions embodied in each of the paradoxes. Everyone involved must constantly wrestle with those tensions and the stress they induce. And the paradoxes never go away—they're at the heart of the innovation process. Thus, they can only be managed but never resolved for good. Knowing about them and why they exist can help, but it doesn't make them easier to deal with.

That's why organizational innovation requires both organizational *willingness* and *ability*. Clearly, any group that wishes to innovate must be *able* to collaborate, experiment, and integrate possible solutions. That is, it must possess the skills to undertake those activities productively. But, given all the barriers to innovation, leaders and their people must also be *willing* to do the hard work of innovation. Successful organizations develop a deep sense of community that helps individuals endure the tensions and stress, and prevents the organization from flying apart due to all the opposing forces at play.

Finally, the paradoxes help explain why leading innovation requires something other than conventional command-and-control leadership—a different way of thinking about the role of the leader. As Andrew Stanton, the Academy Award–winning director of *Finding Nemo*, learned from his mentor, John Lasseter:

> *What I realized . . . is, "Fine, I'm not an auteur. I need to write with other people. I need people to work against. It's not about self-exploration—it's not about me—it's about*

making the best movie possible." And as soon as I admit-
ted that, it was amazing how the crew morale pivoted
and suddenly everyone had my back. If you own the fact
that you don't know what you're doing, then you're still
taking charge, you're still being a director. . . . I learned
that from John [Lasseter] on Toy Story—*every time he got*
confessional and said, "Guys, I think I'm just spinning my
wheels," we'd rise up and solve the problem for him.

Many leaders need to rethink what they do if they want a more innovative organization. It takes a powerful leader to unleash and harness innovation. This power resides in managing paradox rather than controlling destiny.

Adapted from hbr.org, December 12, 2014. Reprint H01QWF

6

Find Innovation Where You Least Expect It

by Tony McCaffrey and Jim Pearson

O n the evening of April 14, 1912, the RMS *Titanic* collided with an iceberg in the North Atlantic and sunk two hours and 40 minutes later. Of its 2,200 passengers and crew, only 705 survived, plucked out of 16 lifeboats by the *Carpathia*. Imagine how many more might have lived if crew members had thought of the iceberg as not just the cause of the disaster but a lifesaving solution. The iceberg rose high above the water and stretched some 400 feet in length. The lifeboats might have ferried people there to look for a flat spot. The *Titanic* itself was navigable for a while and might have been able to pull close enough to the iceberg for people to scramble on. Such a rescue operation was not without precedent: Some 60 years before, 127 of 176 passengers emigrating from Ireland to Canada saved themselves in the Gulf of St. Lawrence by climbing aboard an ice floe.

It's impossible to know if this rescue attempt would have worked. At the least it's an intriguing idea—yet surprisingly difficult to envision. If you were to ask a group of executives, even creative product managers and marketers, to come up with innovative scenarios in which all the *Titanic*'s passengers could have been saved, they would very likely have the same blind spot as the crew. The reason is a common psychological bias—called *functional fixedness*—that limits a person to seeing an object only in the way in which it is traditionally used. In a nautical context, an iceberg is a hazard to be avoided; it's very hard to see it any other way.

When it comes to innovation, businesses are constantly hampered by functional fixedness and other cognitive biases that cause people to overlook elegant solutions hidden in plain sight. We have spent years investigating how innovative designs can be built by harnessing the power of the commonly overlooked. We have identified techniques and tools to help overcome cognitive traps and solve problems in innovative ways—whether conceiving new products, finding novel applications for existing products, or anticipating competitive threats. Using the tools doesn't require special talents or heroic degrees of creativity; taken together, they form a simple, low-cost, systematic way to spur innovation.

To understand how the tools work, let's first look at the three cognitive barriers they address.

Functional Fixedness

In the 1930s, the German psychologist Karl Duncker demonstrated the phenomenon of functional fixedness with a famous brainteaser. He gave subjects a candle, a box of thumbtacks, and a book of matches and asked them to find a way to affix the candle to the wall so that when it was lit, wax would not drip onto the

Idea in Brief

Context

The tendency to fixate on the most common use of an object—a bias researchers call "functional fixedness"—is a serious barrier to innovation. The problem is that we see the object's use rather than the object itself.

Key Idea

We can overcome this bias—and similar biases about the object's design and purpose—by changing how we describe the object and how we think about its component parts.

In Practice

An alternative to brainstorming, which the authors call *brainswarming*, brings these techniques to life.

floor. Many people had a hard time realizing that the answer was to empty the box of tacks, attach the candle to the inside of the box with melted wax, and then tack the box to the wall. The box acts as a shelf that supports the candle and catches the dripping wax. Because the box had been presented to subjects as a tack holder, they couldn't see it any other way.

In similar puzzles—known by cognitive psychologists as "insight problems"—people have trouble seeing that in a pinch a plastic lawn chair could be used as a paddle (turn it over, grab two legs, and start rowing); that a basketball could be deflated, formed into the shape of a bowl, and used to safely carry hot coals from one campsite to another; or that a candlewick could be used to tie things together (scrape the wax away to free the string).

What causes functional fixedness? When we see a common object, we automatically screen out awareness of features that are not important for its use. This is an efficient neurological tactic for everyday life, but it's the enemy of innovation.

Overcoming functional fixedness

Breaking an object down into its component parts can reveal new uses.

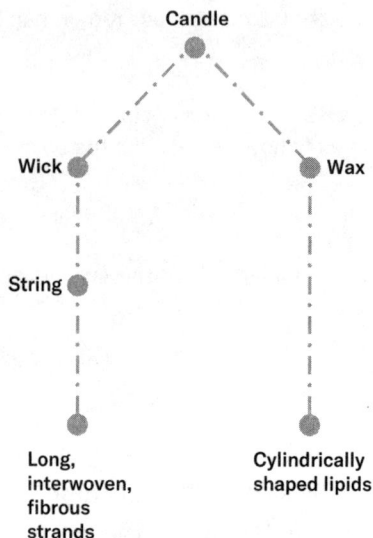

One way to overcome the problem is to change how you describe an object. When told that a candlewick is a string, for instance, almost everyone recognizes that it could be used to tie things together. Our "generic parts technique" is a systematic way to change the way an object is described to avoid unintentionally narrowing people's conception of it, opening them to more ideas for its uses.

We consider each element of an object in turn and ask two questions: "Can it be broken down further?" and "Does our description imply a particular use?" If the answer to either question is yes, we keep breaking down the elements until they're described in their most general terms, mapping the results on a simple tree. When an iceberg is described generically as a floating surface 200 feet to 400 feet long, its potential as a life-saving platform soon emerges. (See the exhibit "Overcoming functional fixedness" for a visualization of the parts of a candle.)

Calling something a "wick" implies its use as a conduit of a flame. Describing it as a "string" strips away a layer of preconceived uses and suggests less common ones. Breaking the string down further into its constituent parts of "fibrous strands" might spark even more uses.

To see if generating generic descriptions bolsters creative thinking, our research team presented two groups of students with eight insight problems that required overcoming the functional fixedness bias in order to solve. We told the members of one group simply to try their best. We taught the other group the generic parts technique and then asked them to use it on the problems. The people in the first group were able to solve, on average, 49% of the problems (just shy of four of them). Those who systematically engaged in creating generic descriptions of their resources were able to solve, on average, 83% (or 6.64) of them.

Design Fixation

Simple insight problems given in a psychology lab can be solved by focusing on only four types of features—materials, size, shape, and parts. But solutions to real-world engineering problems often depend on noticing unusual aspects of a broader range of features. This, as we noted, is very difficult to do.

We studied this phenomenon by asking 15 people to list as many features and associations as they could for a candle, a broom, and a dozen other common objects. We then classified their responses by the type of feature, including its color,

Promising features for a pouch

If you consider an object's less obvious characteristics, new purposes may arise. Some features to consider in the case of a candy pouch are:

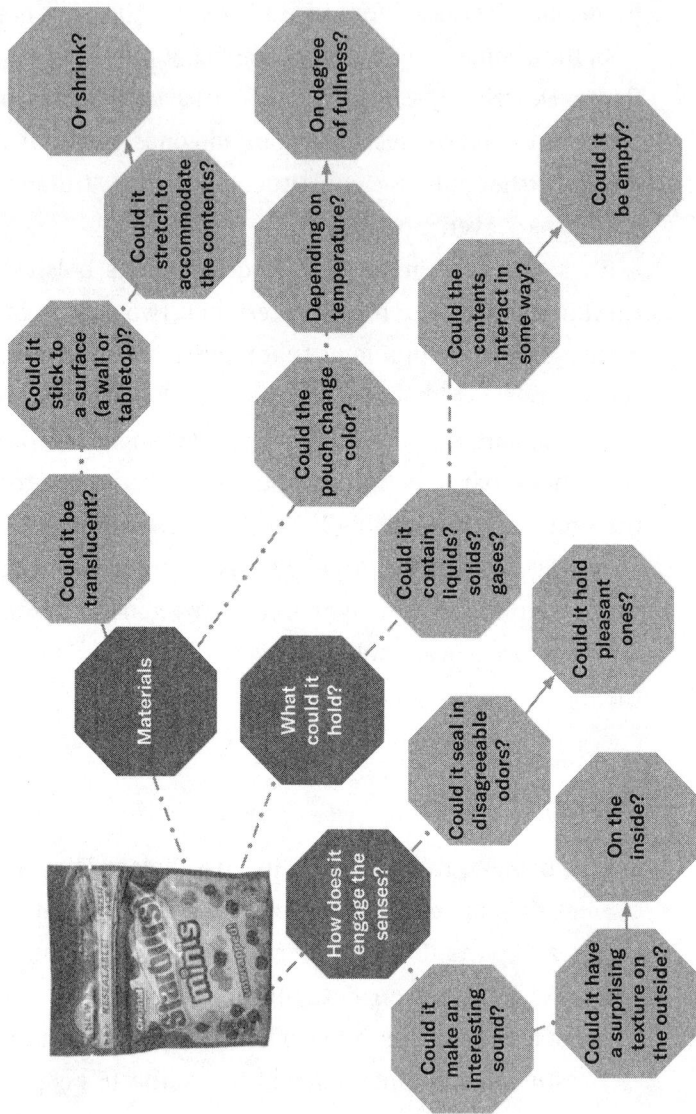

shape, material, designed use, and aesthetic properties, along with the emotions it evokes, the type of energy it generates, and the objects it's commonly paired with. On average, participants overlooked almost 21 of the 32 types of features (about 65%) that we had previously identified for each object.

Why? When handed a product and asked to create a new design or variation on it, people tend to fixate on the features of the current design. This obstacle to novelty is called design fixation. To take a real-world example, when people are shown a sturdy, resealable pouch full of candy and asked to think of a new design that could lead to new uses, they tend to manipulate the types of features used to create the current design—that is, they focus on the width of the base of the pouch or the rigidity of the plastic that makes it stand. To be truly innovative, however, you need to manipulate the features that everyone else has overlooked.

But how do you do that? Just as airline pilots have long used checklists to make sure they don't skip any necessary steps when preparing for flight, we developed a checklist of types of product features that people tend to overlook. Whether your product is a physical object or an intangible process, we recommend that you develop a checklist of features that were important to your previous and current innovation projects and add to the list with each new project. Teams working on innovation projects can then refer to the list to prompt them to consider features they would probably overlook—thus saving time, effort, and frustration. Examining the pouch of candy with our checklist in mind permitted us to easily uncover many features that could lead to new designs and new uses. First, every pouch sold has something in it. This feature is so obvious that its absence is commonly overlooked. Why not sell empty pouches so that customers can decide what to use them for: jewelry, spare change, nuts and bolts, cosmetics, and so on? Imagine empty pouches next to the sandwich bags, freezer bags, and storage bags in your supermarket. Second, most pouches sold are about the size of your hand. Systematically considering changes to the size triggers new ideas for possible contents. What about selling a gallon of paint in a resealable pouch, for instance? Third, current pouches have one inner compartment. But what might you do with more? You could, say, sell two-compartment pouches for things you want to mix together later: cereal in the top compartment and milk in the bottom, salad in the bottom and dressing in the top, and so on. Fourth, consider the pouch as a container of aroma (or as a guard against it). You could sell a large pouch as a garbage can that reseals to keep in the odor. These are just a few of the new designs that emerge from contemplating a checklist of overlooked features.

Goal Fixedness

Suppose we asked you to think of a way to adhere something to a garbage can. Chances are that like most people, you would think of using glue or tape, both forms of adhesives. But what if we asked you instead to *fasten* something to the can? Just switching a specific verb like "adhere" to a more general one would most likely prompt you to list a wider range of possibilities: binder clip, paper clip, nail, string, Velcro, and so on. That's because the way a goal is phrased often narrows people's thinking. We call this barrier "goal fixedness." Framing a problem in more general terms can help overcome it.

But it can be hard to determine what constitutes a "more general term." Is "fasten" more general than "adhere"? A good resource for mapping terms is a thesaurus that makes hierarchical structure

What's in a name?

How broadly—or narrowly—you phrase a goal affects how you visualize it.

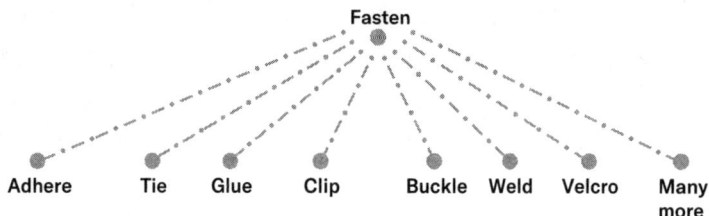

explicit by identifying hyponyms—more-specific synonyms—
for them. For example, the online thesaurus WordNet indicates
that there are least 61 ways to fasten things—including sew,
clamp, chain, garter, strap, hook, staple, belt, screw, wire, buckle,
cement, tack, joggle, button, and rivet. Each describes the concept of fastening one thing to another in a slightly different way
and gives rise to diverse solutions. "Adhere," by contrast, has
only four hyponyms.

Action words, the centerpiece of most goals, often have hyponyms. Each hyponym hints at a more specific way to achieve the
goal. There are 172 for the verb "remove," 50 for "guide," 46 for
"transport," 115 terms for "separate," and—perhaps surprisingly—
only 24 for the seemingly very general term "mix."

Of course, a goal consists of more than just a verb. The verb
expresses what sort of change you're after, but nouns express
what needs changing, and prepositional phrases express important constraints and relationships between things. Put them all
together, and almost any goal can be expressed as a verb (fasten),
a noun (something), and a prepositional phrase (to a garbage
can). Try it: Increase sales in Massachusetts, reduce vibrations

in skis, and so on. By putting your goal in this format and playing with the hyponyms of each of its parts, you can explore diverse approaches to your problem in a simple and cost-effective way.

Here's how the approach worked when one of us (Jim) applied it to the real-world goal to reduce concussions in football. First he dropped the prepositional phrase "in football" from consideration and focused on the verb and noun: "reduce concussions." To break free of hidden assumptions, he used WordNet to rephrase the goal in as many different ways as possible: lessen trauma, weaken crash, soften jolt, reduce energy, absorb energy, minimize force, exchange forces, substitute energy, oppose energy, repel energy, lessen momentum, and so on. Using Google, he performed searches such as "concussions lessen trauma" to see which ways of phrasing the goal had been heavily explored already and which ones were under-explored.

Jim found that in the context of concussions, the phrase "repel energy" had relatively few search results—a sign that the solution it implied might have been overlooked. One way to repel energy is through magnets, and this suggested a possible approach: Make each helmet magnetic with the same pole so that two helmets would repel each other when in close proximity. Results from initial tests showed that when the helmets were about to collide, they decelerated, and because of their circular shape, they tended to glance off each other, as two magnetic billiard balls would, rather than smashing head-on. Several physicists have verified the plausibility of this approach for significantly reducing the force during helmet collisions.

We began the patenting process for our solution, but our lawyer discovered that someone had submitted the same idea just weeks earlier. We tip our hat to that person.

Visualizing Innovative Thinking

At its most basic level, problem-solving consists of two connected activities: framing a goal and combining resources to accomplish it. Each variation of the goal, and every discovery of a "hidden" feature of an available resource, can suggest a different course to take. Our approach involves mapping the relationships among all the possibilities in a simple graph, somewhat analogous to a decision tree.

Starting with the goal at the top, we represent each refinement of the goal as a vector pointing downward. The available resources are placed at the bottom, with their features extending upward. Interactions among the resources and their features

---

Dominant survival strategy on the *Titanic*

The first step in discovering how resources could be used to reach a goal is to map the most obvious solution.

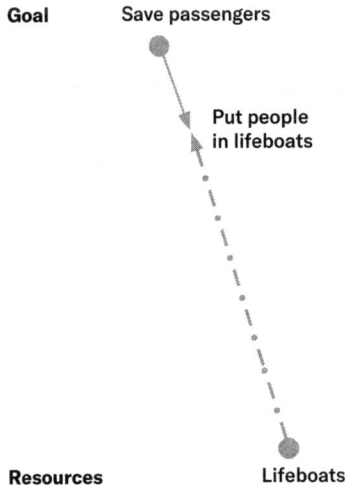

Goal   Save passengers

Put people
in lifeboats

Resources   Lifeboats

A Smarter Way to Brainstorm

When people generate "brainswarming" graphs together, it's best for the group to work initially in silence, write contributions on sticky notes, and place the sticky notes at the proper place on the ever-growing graph. The benefits of silence include the following:

- The talkative few cannot dominate the session.

- There's no need for a facilitator to keep people from hijacking the discussion or judging others.

- People can work in parallel, so ideas are generated faster.

- No one needs to create a summary of the session. Take a picture of the graph and distribute it by email, or just keep the graph up on the wall for later use.

- There's no need to group similar ideas together, as you would in a traditional brainstorming session, because the grouping is done as the graph is built.

- Ideas are concise, since all contributions must fit on a sticky note.

- The silence allows people to move between thinking, writing down ideas, placing them on the graph, and building on one another's ideas.

- Top-down (big-picture) thinkers can work side by side with bottom-up (detail-oriented) thinkers.

- Fear of judgment from the boss or colleagues is reduced.

- There's no need for everyone to be present at the same time during the session. The graph can remain on the wall so that people can contribute at different times. Online brainswarming allows groups from around the world to work together remotely.

Overlooked strategies for saving *Titanic* passengers

Find new ways to name the goal, and new resources may present themselves.

extend further toward the top. When the two sets of vectors connect, we have a "solution path." A solution path can be built by working from the top down, from the bottom up, or by switching back and forth between considering the goal and thinking about the resources.

This approach is an effective alternative to traditional brainstorming sessions for group innovation work, because it allows people to play to their strengths: Strategically oriented people can focus on refining the goal, while those more familiar with technologies and production processes can begin with the resources. We call this approach *brainswarming*—a nod to the concept of swarm intelligence. As people contribute to the growing graph, their activity resembles a swarm of insects.

To understand how this works, let's return to the problem facing the passengers on the *Titanic*. We'll start with the goal "save passengers." The most obvious resources are the lifeboats. The simplest application of the resources to achieve the goal is "put people in the lifeboats." Thus, we begin with a straight line (see the exhibit "Dominant survival strategy on the *Titanic*").

Next, we find different ways to phrase the goal to bring out different solutions. For instance, slightly different goals would be "keep people warm and breathing" and "keep people out of the water." Let's look more closely at one of the options: keep people out of the water. One way is to place them on floating things—not just lifeboats—which might spark a fuller consideration of the resources at hand. You might remember that wood floats, for instance, suggesting that wooden tables might have been of help. Planks, or perhaps doors, from the ship might have been placed between the lifeboats to hold more people out of the water.

Moving from floating things to even more-general considerations of buoyancy might bring to mind the many steamer trunks on board. Tying a set of trunks together to produce another sort of makeshift floating platform might have been enough to support several people directly or to provide a foundation upon which to build a more secure platform of wooden planks.

It was estimated that as many as 40 cars were on board. That means 160 tires and inner tubes (not to mention spare tires) were at passengers' disposal. Tying together rubber tires and inner tubes might conceivably have created a floating raft on which wooden boards could have been placed. And of course, the iceberg itself is a giant floating thing.

On that April night in 1912, none of these ideas might have worked, particularly since it took so long for people to understand the peril they were in. But the point of such an exercise is not to discover the "right solution"; it is to uncover as many connections between the goal and the widest view of the features of available resources as possible so that people look beyond the obvious.

The goal of the brainswarming graph, therefore, is to distill the problem-solving process to its most basic components and show how they are all related to one another. People do not have to remember all the components under consideration, because the graph shows them in a glance. This systematic approach takes some of the mystery out of innovation.

. . .

In our research, we are discovering that barriers to innovation are like gravity—pervasive, predictable, and not all that strong. There are many ways to overcome them, but the simplest and easiest path is to help your innovators notice what they're overlooking. Often it's right in front of their eyes.

Originally published in December 2015. Reprint R1512F

7

Engineering Reverse Innovations

by Amos Winter and Vijay Govindarajan

Slowly but steadily, it's dawning on Western multinationals that it may be a good idea to design products and services in developing economies and, after adding some global tweaks, export them to developed countries.

This process, called "reverse innovation" because it's the opposite of the traditional approach of creating products for advanced economies first, allows companies to enjoy the best of both worlds. It was first described six years ago in an HBR article cowritten by one of the authors of this article, Vijay Govindarajan.

But despite the inexorable logic of reverse innovation, only a few multinationals—notably Coca-Cola, GE, Harmon, Microsoft, Nestlé, PepsiCo, Procter & Gamble, Renault, and Levi Strauss— have succeeded in crafting products in emerging markets and selling them worldwide. Even emerging giants—such as Jain Irrigation, Mahindra & Mahindra, and the Tata Group—have found it tough to create offerings that catch on in both kinds of markets.

For three years now we've been studying this challenge, analyzing more than 35 reverse innovation projects started by multinationals. Our research suggests that the problem stems from a failure to grasp the unique economic, social, and technical contexts of emerging markets. At most Western companies, product developers, who spend a lifetime creating offerings for people similar to themselves, lack a visceral understanding of emerging-market consumers, whose spending habits, use of technologies, and perceptions of status are very different. Executives have trouble figuring out how to overcome the constraints of emerging markets—or take advantage of the freedoms they offer. Unable to find the way forward, they tend to fall into one or more mental traps that prevent them from successfully developing reverse innovations.

Our study also shows that executives can avoid these traps by adhering to certain design principles, which together provide a road map for reverse innovation. We distilled them partly from our work with multinationals and partly from the firsthand experiences of a team of MIT engineers led by this article's other author, Amos Winter. His team spent six years designing an off-road wheelchair for people in developing countries, which is now manufactured in India. Called the Leveraged Freedom Chair (LFC), it is 80% faster and 40% more efficient to propel than a conventional wheelchair, and it sells for approximately $250—on par with other developing world wheelchairs. The technologies that generate its high performance and low cost have been incorporated into a Western version, the GRIT Freedom Chair, which was modified with consumer feedback and sells in the United States for $3,295—less than half the price of competing products.

As we will show in the following pages, the reverse innovation process succeeds when engineering creatively intersects with strategy. Companies can capture business opportunities

Idea in Brief

The Problem

Multinational companies are starting to realize that developing new products in and for emerging markets will allow them to outperform local rivals and undercut them on price—and even disrupt Western markets. However, most struggle to create those products and then sell them in the developed world.

The Analysis

A three-year study suggests that Western companies often fail to grasp the economic, social, and technical contexts of emerging markets. Most Western product engineers find it tough to overcome these markets' constraints and leverage their flexibility. They tend to fall into one or more traps that thwart their innovation efforts.

The Takeaways

Companies can avoid these traps if they:

1. Define the problem independent of solutions.
2. Create the optimal solution using the design flexibility available.
3. Understand the technical landscape behind the problem.
4. Test products with as many stakeholders as possible.
5. Use constraints to create global winners.

only when they design appropriate products or services and understand the business case for them. That's why it took two academics—one teaching mechanical engineering, and the other strategy—to come up with the principles that must guide the creation of reverse innovations.

Five Traps—and How to Avoid Them

For every product, multinational companies typically produce three variations: a top-of-the-line offering, which provides the best performance at a premium price; a "better" version, which delivers 80% of that performance at 80% of the price; and a "good" variant, which provides 70% and costs 70% as much. To break into emerging markets, where consumers have very high expectations but much smaller pocketbooks, multinationals usually follow a design philosophy that minimizes the up-front risks: They value-engineer the "good" product, watering it down to a "fair" one that offers 50% of the performance at 50% of the price.

This rarely works. In developing countries, not only do "fair" (or "good enough") products prove too expensive for the middle class, but the upmarket consumers—who can afford them—will prefer the top-of-the-line versions. Meanwhile, because of economies of scale and the globalization of supply chains, local companies are now bringing out high-value products, at relatively cheap prices, more quickly than they used to. Consequently, most multinationals capture only small slivers of the local market.

To win over consumers in developing countries, multinationals' products and services must match or beat the performance of existing ones but at a lower cost. In other words, they must provide 100% of the performance at 10% of the price, as product developers wryly put it. Only through the creation of such disruptive products and technologies can companies both outperform local rivals and undercut them on price. But the traps we mentioned earlier prevent companies from meeting this challenge. To escape those traps, they must follow five design principles.

Trap 1: Trying to match market segments to existing products

Current offerings and processes cast a long shadow when multinationals start creating products for developing countries. At first it appears to be quicker, cheaper, and less risky to adapt an existing product than to develop one from scratch. The idea that time-tested products, with modifications, won't appeal to lower-income customers is difficult to digest. Designers struggle to get away from existing technologies.

The U.S. tractor-manufacturer John Deere, a seasoned global player, encountered this problem in India. There Deere initially sold tractors it had carefully modified for emerging markets. But its small tractors had a wide turning radius, because they had been designed for America's large farms. Indian holdings are very small and close to one another, so farmers there prefer tractors that can make narrow turns. Only after John Deere designed ab initio a tractor for the local market did it taste success in India.

Design principle 1: Define the problem independent of solutions

Casting off preconceived solutions before you set down to define problems will help your company avoid the first trap—and spot opportunities outside its existing product portfolio. Consider the problem of irrigating farms in emerging markets. Farmers will argue for the expansion of the power grid so that they can use electricity to run water pumps and irrigate fields. However, farmers need water, not electricity, and the real requirement is getting water to crops—not power to pumps. If they isolate the problem, engineers may find that creating ponds near fields or using solar-powered pumps is more cost-effective and environmentally appropriate than expanding the power grid.

When defining problems, executives must keep their eyes and ears open for behavior that may signal needs that customers haven't articulated. In 2002, Commonwealth Telecommunications Organisation researchers reported that in East Africa people were transferring airtime to family and friends in villages, who were then using or reselling it. Doing so allowed workers in cities to get money to people back home without making long and unsafe journeys with large amounts of cash. It indicated a latent demand for money remittance services. That's how M-Pesa, the successful mobile money-transfer service, was born.

It's good to study the global market in-depth before kicking off the design process. For example, when the MIT team analyzed the wheelchair market, it learned that of the 40 million people with disabilities who didn't have wheelchairs, 70% lived in rural areas where rough roads and muddy paths were often the only links to education, employment, markets, and the community. Environmental conditions were harsh; traditional wheelchairs broke down quickly as a result and were difficult to repair. Because of their poverty, most people got wheelchairs free or at subsidized prices from NGOs, religious organizations, or government agencies. Those suppliers were willing to pay $250 to $350 for a wheelchair—an important price constraint.

No wheelchair user specified the mobility solution they desired; the team had to figure out the needs of the market by watching and listening. For inspiration, it drew on the numerous complaints it heard: Wheelchairs were tough to push on village roads; manually powered tricycles were too big to use indoors; imported wheelchairs couldn't be repaired in villages; the commute to an office was often more than a mile, so it was tiring. And so on.

The team's assessment of consumer needs generated four core design requirements:

1. A price of approximately $250

2. A travel range of three miles a day over varied terrain

3. Indoor usability and maneuverability

4. Easy, low-cost maintenance and local repair

Key advantages of the Leveraged Freedom Chair

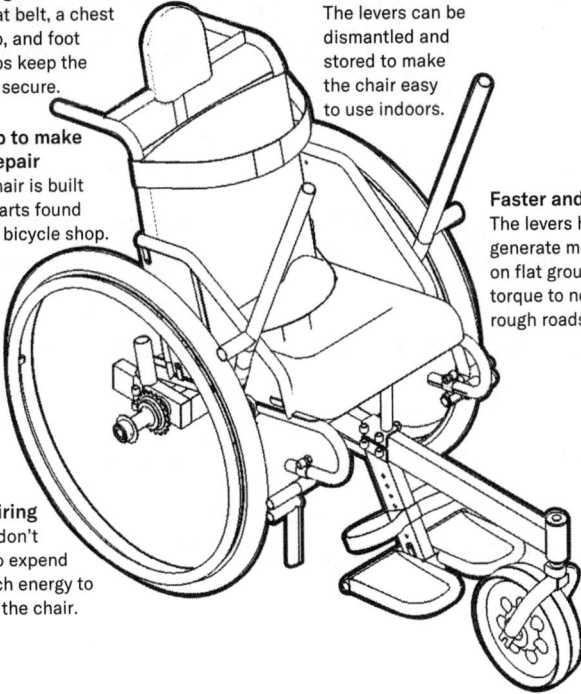

Extra safe
A long wheelbase, a seat belt, a chest strap, and foot straps keep the user secure.

Cheap to make and repair
The chair is built with parts found at any bicycle shop.

Versatile
The levers can be dismantled and stored to make the chair easy to use indoors.

Faster and all-terrain
The levers help users generate more speed on flat ground or torque to negotiate rough roads.

Less tiring
Users don't have to expend as much energy to propel the chair.

Source: GRIT/Asme Demand

Those criteria conveyed little about what form the wheelchair would have to take. However, had the team missed one of them, imposed an existing solution, or made its own assumptions, it probably would have failed.

Trap 2: Trying to reduce the price by eliminating features

Many multinationals think this is the way to make products afford-able for consumers in emerging markets. People in developing countries are willing to accept lower quality and products based on sunset technologies, runs the argument. This approach often leads to poor decisions and bad product designs.

For example, when one of the Big Three automobile makers decided to enter India in the mid-1990s, it charged its product developers in Detroit with coming up with a suitable model. The designers took an existing mid-price car and eliminated what they felt were unnecessary features for India, including power windows in the rear doors. The new model's price was within the reach of Indians at the top of the pyramid—who hire chauffeurs. Thus the chauffeurs got power windows up front while the owners had to hand-crank the rear windows, greatly reducing customer satisfaction.

Design principle 2: Create an optimal solution, not a watered-down one, using the design freedoms available in emerging markets

Though emerging markets have many constraints, they offer intrinsic design freedoms as well. These freedoms take various forms: In Egypt high irradiance makes solar power attractive in areas with unreliable power; in India low labor costs and high material costs make manual fabrication cost-effective. Even behavioral differences broaden companies' options: some African consumers prioritize the purchase of TV sets over roofs, suggesting that companies must appeal to users' wants as well as their needs.

Carefully considering design freedoms helped the MIT team achieve many objectives. For instance, wheelchairs that use a mechanical system of multiple gears, just as geared bicycles do, were available in the developing world, but they were very expensive, and few could afford them. Compelled to devise an alternative, the engineers homed in on people's ability to make a broad range of arm movements as something they could use in the drivetrain to make the chair go faster or slower. While that ability isn't specific to emerging markets, the engineers wouldn't have thought of using it if they weren't trying to achieve high performance at a low price—a requirement specific to emerging markets.

The MIT team designed the LFC with two long levers that are pushed to propel the chair; users change speed by shifting the position of their hands on the levers. To go up a hill, users grab high on the levers and gain more leverage; in "low gear" the levers provide 50% more torque than pushing the rims of the chair does. On a flat road, they grab low and push through a larger angle to move faster, generating speeds that are 75% faster than a standard wheelchair's. To brake, users pull back on the levers.

By making the users the machines' most complex part—they are both the power source and the gearbox—the team could fabricate the drivetrain from a simple, single-speed assembly of bicycle parts. In fact, the ability to use bicycle parts was another freedom the team could exploit. People in developing countries use bicycles extensively, and repair shops that stock spare parts are almost everywhere. Incorporating bicycle parts into the drivetrain made the LFC low cost, sustainable, and easy to repair, especially in remote villages.

Trap 3: Forgetting to think through all the technical requirements of emerging markets

When designing offerings for the developing world, engineers assume they're dealing with the same technical landscape that they are in the developed world. But while the laws of science may be the same everywhere, the technical infrastructure is very different in emerging markets. Engineers must understand the technical factors behind problems there—the physics, the chemistry, the energetics, the ecology, and so on—and conduct rigorous analyses to determine the viability of possible solutions.

Thorough calculations will allow engineers to validate or refute assumptions about the market. Consider the PlayPump, designed for Africa, which pumps water from the ground into a tower by harnessing the energy of village children pushing a merry-go-round. Having children do something useful for the community while playing is a win-win by any yardstick. Moreover, a first-order engineering analysis suggested that the technological assumptions were logical.

Let's assume that in a 1,000-strong village, each person needs three liters of drinking water a day, the village has a tower that can hold 3,000 liters, and it's 10 meters high. Using high school physics, one can calculate that 25 children, playing for 10 minutes each, could theoretically fill the tower.

But further analysis alters the picture. After all, children spin merry-go-rounds so that they can ride them until they're dizzy, and if all the energy from their pushing goes to pumping water, the merry-go-round will stop as soon as they stop pushing. That's no fun! If we assume that half their energy goes into spinning and half into pumping, the energy requirement doubles; 50 children must use the PlayPump for 10 minutes each daily to keep the tower full.

If the water comes from a well 10 meters deep, double the energy will be necessary and 100 children must use the merry-go-round. Accounting for inefficiencies, the number could go to 200. What happens when it's too hot, wet, or cold, and children don't want to play on the PlayPump? How will the village get its water then? If the makers of the PlayPump had included all those factors in their calculations, they would have realized it wasn't

U.S.-focused upgrades to the GRIT Freedom Chair

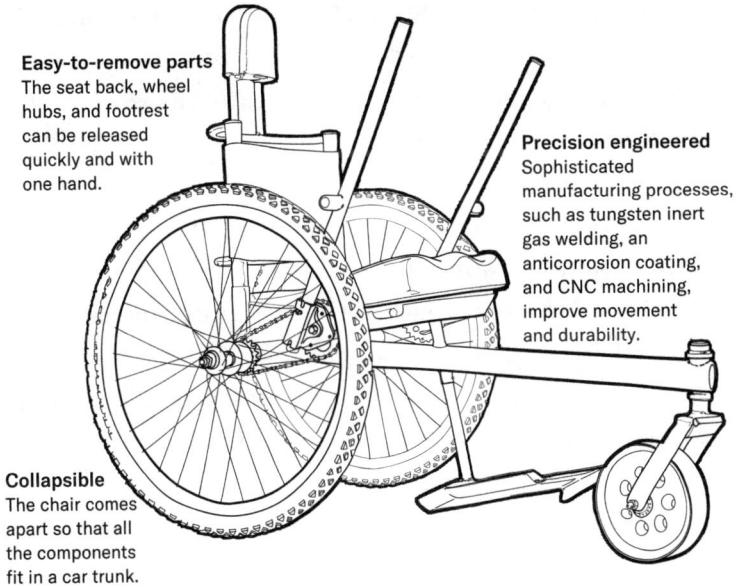

Easy-to-remove parts
The seat back, wheel hubs, and footrest can be released quickly and with one hand.

Precision engineered
Sophisticated manufacturing processes, such as tungsten inert gas welding, an anticorrosion coating, and CNC machining, improve movement and durability.

Collapsible
The chair comes apart so that all the components fit in a car trunk.

Source: GRIT/Nathan Cooke

a technically viable solution. Despite receiving the World Bank Development Marketplace award in 2000 and donor pledges of $16.4 million in 2006, PlayPumps International had stopped installing new units by 2010. The PlayPump sounded like a good idea, but a village water system needs reliable power—and ensuring that isn't child's play.

Design principle 3: Analyze the technical landscape behind the consumer problem

Underlying technical relationships may look markedly different in developing countries. For example, urban Indian homes receive water from pressurized municipal supply systems, just like those found in the United States, which ensure that if there is a leak, water goes out but contaminants can't get in. However, most Indian households use booster pumps to suck water from the municipal pipes to rooftop tanks. This suction pulls contaminants from the ground into the pipes, creating a mechanism for contamination that is not common in the United States.

Social and economic factors often drive the technical requirements for products. For instance, if a company wants to sell inexpensive tractors to low-income farmers, it must make them light; material costs determine much of a tractor's price. Engineers then must check how lowering the weight would affect the machine's performance, particularly traction and pulling force. The latter is important; in emerging markets, farmers use tractors not only to farm but for odd jobs, such as transporting people.

By studying the technical landscape, engineers can identify pain points as well as creative paths around them. Understanding the requirements for energy, force, heat transfer, and so on will illuminate novel ways of satisfying them. As noted earlier, the LFC is human powered, which eliminates the costs of a motor and an energy source. However, the design team had to figure out how users' upper body strength could provide propulsion. It did so by calculating the power and force that people could produce with their arms and the amounts needed on various kinds of terrain. Finally, the designers worked out the optimal length of the two levers so that users could travel at peak efficiency across normal terrain and have enough strength to propel their way out of trouble in harsh conditions such as mud or sand.

Trap 4: Neglecting stakeholders

Many multinationals seem to think that all they need to do to educate product designers about consumers' needs and desires is to parachute them into an emerging market for a few days; drive them around a couple of cities, villages, and slums; and allow them to observe the locals. Those perceptions will be enough to develop products that people will purchase, they assume. But nothing could be further from the truth.

Design principle 4: Test products with as many stakeholders as possible

Companies would do well to map out the entire chain of stakeholders who will determine a product's success, at the beginning of the design process. In addition to asking who the end user will be and what they need, companies must consider who will make the product, distribute it, sell it, pay for it, repair it, and dispose of it. This will help in developing not just the product but also a scalable business model.

It's best to adopt the attitude that you're designing with, not for, stakeholders. If treated as equals, they're more likely to participate in the process and provide honest feedback. When you're designing a prosthetic limb, for instance, collaborate with amputees, the clinics that provide the prostheses, and the organizations that pay for them. If you're able-bodied, it doesn't matter how many doctoral degrees you've earned; you still don't know what it's like to live with a prosthetic device in a developing country.

The MIT team formed partnerships with wheelchair builders and users throughout the developing world. Those stakeholders, who provided insights on how to make the wheelchair better, easier to manufacture, more robust, and cheaper, came up with ideas for several features. The team gathered further feedback through field trials in East Africa, Guatemala, and India, conducted in conjunction with local wheelchair manufacturing and supply organizations. The tests had a huge impact, resulting in several design modifications.

Although the first prototype performed well on rough terrain in East Africa, it didn't do so well indoors. It was too wide to go through a standard doorway, which the MIT designers hadn't noticed, and it was 20 pounds heavier than rival products were. For the next iteration, tested in Guatemala, the engineers reduced the chair's width by shaping the seat closer to the user's hips, bringing the wheels closer to the frame, and using narrower tires. By conducting a structural analysis, optimizing the strength-to-weight ratio of the frame, and reducing materials wherever possible, the team also decreased the LFC's weight by 20 pounds. That version performed well indoors, but several users felt they might fall out when traversing rough terrain. So the team included foot, waist, and chest straps to secure the user to the seat in tests in India. Users rated the third version at par with conventional wheelchairs indoors and far superior outdoors.

No matter how thorough engineers are, users expose design flaws that only they can notice. For instance, of the seven major improvements users suggested, only eliminating the LFC's excess weight had been evident to the MIT team before the East African trial. It's critical to test prototypes in the field with potential users and design solutions with organizations that will disseminate the product. Remember, design is iterative; you can't get it right the first time, so be prepared to test many prototypes.

Trap 5: Refusing to believe that products designed for emerging markets could have global appeal

Western companies tend to assume that consumers in developed markets, who are brand-conscious and performance-sensitive, will never want products from emerging markets, even if their prices are lower. Executives also worry that even if those products did catch on, they could be dangerous, cannibalizing higher-priced, higher-margin offerings.

Design principle 5: Use emerging-market constraints to create global winners

Before designing solutions, companies should identify the inherent constraints that will operate on the new product or service—such as low average consumer income, poor infrastructure, and limited natural resources. This list will dictate the requirements—like price, durability, and materials—that new designs must meet.

The constraints of developing countries usually force technological breakthroughs that help innovations crack global markets. The new products become platforms on which companies can add features and capabilities that will delight many tiers of consumers across the world. One example is the Logan, a car Renault designed specifically for Eastern European customers, who are price-sensitive and demand value. Launched in Romania in 2004, the Logan cost only $6,500 but offered greater size and trunk space, higher ground clearance, and more reliability than rival products. To ensure a low price, Renault used fewer parts than usual in the vehicle and manufactured it in Romania, where labor costs are relatively low.

Two years later, Renault decided to make the Logan attractive to consumers in developed markets, by adding more safety features and greater cosmetic appeal, including metallic colors. In France it sold the Logan for as much as $9,400. In Germany sales of the Logan jumped from 6,000 units to 85,000 units over a three-year period. By 2013 sales in Western Europe had reached 430,000 units—a 19% increase over 2012. Thus, while the constraints in Eastern Europe forced Renault to create a new auto design, the result was a product that delivered high value at low cost to consumers in Western Europe as well.

Something similar is happening with the LFC: Wheelchair users in the United States and Europe have noticed the media buzz about the product and want to buy it. The MIT team worked with Continuum, a Boston-based design studio, to conduct a study of what a U.S. version of the LFC could look like. The designers also tested the LFC with potential customers in the West to identify features to add. The GRIT Freedom Chair, as the developed world model is called, was designed to fit into car trunks in the United States. It also has quick-release wheels that users can remove with one hand and is made from bicycle parts available in the United States.

Although commercial production of the Freedom Chair began only in May 2015, it's on its way to success in the developed world. The venture the MIT team founded to make the chairs, Global Research Innovation and Technology, was one of four startups that received a diamond award at MassChallenge, the world's largest startup competition, three years ago. In 2014, GRIT ran a Kickstarter campaign to launch the Freedom Chair, meeting its funding goal in only five days.

How the Principles Pay Off

Few companies have avoided the traps we've described as well as the global shaving products giant Gillette did when designing an offering for India. As recently as a decade ago, Gillette made most of its money in that country by catering to top-of-the-pyramid consumers with pricey products. In 2005, Procter & Gamble acquired Gillette and immediately saw an opportunity to expand market share in the country.

Prodded by its new parent, which had been in India since the early 1990s, Gillette decided to develop a product for the 400 million middle-income Indians who shave primarily with double-edge razors. It began by exploring consumer requirements. After mapping out the value chain, from steel suppliers to end users, a cross-functional team conducted ethnographic research, spending over 3,000 hours with 1,000 would-be consumers.

Gillette learned that the needs of Indian shavers differ from those of their developed world counterparts in four ways:

Affordability

The price would be a critical constraint, since Gillette's main competitor, the double-edge razor, costs just Re 1 (less than 2 cents).

Safety

Consumers in this market segment sit on the floor in the dark early-morning hours and, using a small amount of still water, wield a mirror in one hand and a razor in the other. Shaving often results in nicks and cuts, because double-edge razors don't have a protective layer between the blade and the skin.

Even so, when Gillette's product designers watched Indian men shaving, most of the men did not cut themselves. Their response was simple: "We are experts; we don't cut ourselves." However, the team concluded that shaving requires concentration; Indian shavers could not relax or talk during the process for fear of injuring themselves. Gillette had identified a latent need: Most shavers were keen to relieve the tension by using a safer razor and blade.

Ease of use

Indian men have heavier beards and thicker facial hair than most American men do, and shave less frequently, so they have to tackle longer hairs. They also like to use a lot of shaving cream. All of that leads their razors to clog up quickly. With little running water at their disposal, Indian men need razors that they can easily rinse.

Close shaves

Gillette rightly assumed that Indian men want close shaves, as men across the world do, but the difference is that they do not place a premium on time. They spend up to 30 minutes shaving, whereas U.S. men spend five to seven minutes.

To come up with a competitive product, Gillette had to relearn the science of shaving with a single blade. It found that multiple passes of a single-blade razor can achieve a close shave because of the viscoelastic nature of hair. As a blade cuts strands of hair, it also pulls them out a little from the skin. The hairs don't spring back at once; the follicles act like the mechanisms that close a screen door slowly. Because the hairs continue to protrude, the next pass of the blade can cut them a little shorter. And so on.

This process helped Gillette hit upon a valuable design freedom: It could use only a single blade in its new razor, which drastically lowered the production cost. The new razor would also need 80% fewer parts than other razors did, greatly reducing manufacturing complexity.

Gillette's engineers then had to figure out how to flatten the skin before cutting the hairs to ensure a close shave without injury. They also had to understand the mechanics of flushing out the razor by swishing it in a cup of water. Finally, they had to balance competing requirements: Small teeth at the cartridge's front were necessary to flatten the skin before it made contact with the blade, while the rear had to have an unobstructed pass-through to allow hair and shaving cream to wash out easily.

Rethinking the razor from the ground up, the Gillette team also designed a unique pivoting head. That helped the user maneuver around the curves of the face and neck, particularly under the chin—an area difficult to shave. Seeing that Indians gripped razors in numerous ways, Gillette created a bulging handle and textured it to prevent slippage.

Gillette didn't stop at designing a product specifically for India; it also built a new business model to support it. To reduce production and transportation costs, it manufactures the product at several locations. And because India's distribution infrastructure consists of millions of mom-and-pop retailers, the team designed packaging that consumers could easily spot in any store.

Over time the American company did well in this Indian segment—mainly because it didn't set out to make the cheapest razor; it strove to make a product with superior value at an ultralow cost. The Gillette Guard razor costs Rs 15 (around 25 cents)—3% as much as the company's Mach3 razor and 2% as much as its Fusion Power razor—and each refill blade costs Rs 5 (8 cents). Introduced in 2010, the innovative product has quickly gained market share: Two out of three razors sold in India today are Gillette Guards. Although Gillette has not sold the Guard outside India yet, it embodies the promise of a successful reverse innovation.

. . .

Though most Western companies know that the business world has changed dramatically in the past 15 years, they still don't realize that its center of gravity has pretty much shifted to emerging markets. China, India, Brazil, Russia, and Mexico are all likely to be among the world's 12 largest economies by 2030, and any company that wants to remain a market leader will have to focus on consumers there. Chief executives have no choice but to start investing in the infrastructure, processes, and people needed to develop products in emerging markets. Doing so will also allow multinationals to benefit from the "frugal engineering" (as Renault's CEO Carlos Ghosn labeled it) that's possible there. Because of abundant skilled talent—especially engineers—and relatively low salaries in those countries, the costs of creating products there are often lower than in developed nations. But no amount of investment will result in portfolios of successful new products and services if companies don't follow the design principles that govern the development of reverse innovations.

Originally published in July–August 2015. Reprint R1507F

Can AI Help Your Company Innovate? It Depends

by Lynn Wu and Sam Ransbotham

At some point, just about every company must deal with a hard truth: Products get old. It isn't so much that there's a precise expiration date, after which your offerings are suddenly dated. But often, leaders have a moment when they recognize that a product line is getting long in the tooth and realize it's time for a refresh—even if it's still thriving and popular. With the substantial development timelines of many modern complex products, failing to innovate to counter the subtle creep of obsolescence can turn a leader into a laggard.

However, innovation is tough. Corporate innovation is lagging, and innovation in general has largely declined in both quality and quantity. According to recent research, the disruptiveness of scientific paper production dropped between 91% and 100% from 1945 and 2010, and, similarly, the disruptiveness of patenting fell between 78% and 92% during the same time period.[1] But despite these declining rates, scientific knowledge in many fields has become so large, so diverse, and so overlapping that keeping up is incredibly challenging.

Companies need new ways to innovate quickly, cheaply, and productively. Many, quite reasonably, wonder how deploying AI might help. To investigate, we researched how companies are using AI for innovation and found that tools are just tools—success depends on how organizations use these new tools now at their disposal.

Why Products Become Obsolete—and What Companies Need to Do to Stay Current

There are many paths to obsolescence.

First, products can have long developments but short lives. For example, new breakthrough drugs have relatively brief windows before imitators start eroding market share and profitability. Chronic myeloid leukemia (CML), a rare blood cancer, had a poor diagnosis before 2001, when Novartis discovered Gleevec (imatinib), the first effective treatment for CML. But only a few short years later, in 2006, Bristol-Myers Squibb and Otsuka received U.S. Food and Drug Administration (FDA) approval for Sprycel (dasatinib), a similarly effective inhibitor for treating CML. In 2012, Novo Nordisk began developing the blockbuster drugs for weight loss, Ozempic and Wegovy (both semaglutide), receiving FDA approval in 2017 (Ozempic) and 2021 (Wegovy). Now, these drugs generate 52% of Novo Nordisk's total revenue. But in the future?[2] The May 2022 approval of Eli Lilly's Mounjaro, twice as effective for weight loss as Ozempic, already threatens that revenue stream.[3]

Idea in Brief

The Situation

Companies need new ways to innovate quickly, cheaply, and productively. Many are looking to AI for help. Are they right to do so?

The Research

The authors found that success depends on how organizations use the new tools at their disposal. Their studies suggest that firms that have focused on process innovation and innovation by diverse recombination (using a wide variety of technology elements in new ways) may benefit most from the advanced data capabilities of machine learning and AI. Conversely, using AI is less helpful for incremental innovation and making small improvements to existing products, and is almost no help at all for radical innovation.

Second, business contexts change and require more from products. For example, Cooper Standard supplies materials that car manufacturers use to create seals around car doors and windows. But as the electric car market has grown, the company has found that it now needs to meet higher standards. Absent the roar of a gasoline engine, "other sources of noise become more prevalent, and the largest one of those is the noise coming in due to wind around your doors and windows," Chris Couch, SVP and chief technology officer at Cooper Standard, said during a podcast interview with one of us (Ransbotham).[4] Though Cooper Standard's sealants worked well for older noisier cars, newer quieter electric models demand even greater performance. Products that once fit a market well must adapt as market conditions change.

Third, potential combinations are exploding. Car manufacturers depend on the tire manufacturing company Pirelli to provide tires that meet specific performance criteria for new car models. But developing new tires is complex, involving more than 200 different materials and substances.[5] The number of possible combinations is staggering, and working through them all by trial and error would require substantial time, incur considerable costs, and produce a deluge of abandoned prototypes. With a wealth of new materials and new techniques but decreasing lead times, companies need faster ways to explore search space.

Can AI help with these problems? Maybe. While we have seen amazing AI-enabled innovations—from developing new drugs to designing new car chassis—it isn't clear yet how using AI analytics can really help firms improve their innovation.[6] On the one hand, AI models that ingest and synthesize vast data could manage more information than people, which could help with the problem of information overload. And with increased complexity in products and materials, algorithms can predict performance and help reduce search space before investing time and resources in every possible combination. On the other hand, algorithms and data are inherently backward-facing. Complex problems with no known solution may not yet have the data or sufficient data on which to conduct analysis.

Our research shows exemplars using these tools well and evidence of mixed results from a broad sample of other organizations. The new AI tools can help with innovation activities, but they are not panaceas.

Focus on Recombination, Not Radical Reinvention

We have seen some success in addressing these common problems with AI. Fast response? Dave Johnson at Moderna credits the use of AI with helping the company crank out vaccine candidates "as quickly and safely as possible."[7] Context change? At Cooper Standard, they developed AI models to advise chemists on the next set of recipes to try as they iterate toward a new polymer that is already paying off—Couch claimed reductions in R&D design feedback loops of 70% to 80%.[8] Combinatoric explosion? At Pirelli, scientists use AI algorithms to assist human decision-making in selecting new materials for creating tires.[9]

That said, we wondered whether the Moderna, Cooper Standard, and Pirelli examples were anomalies of AI use. To investigate, we built on two studies: first, a survey of 331 firms for practices on process improvement and new technology development, and second, an archival analysis of patent data on new technology development for a broader sample of more than 2,000 publicly traded firms.[10]

Our results indicate that using AI can help firms innovate by exploring wide combinations from a diverse set of technologies. Using AI helps overcome critical barriers in assessing these combinations, such as when knowledge is dispersed throughout a siloed organization. Specifically, our research finds that advanced data capabilities are more likely to be present in firms that (1) orient themselves around process improvement and (2) create new technologies by combining a diverse set of existing technologies than in firms that focus on generating entirely new technologies. And it isn't just that these AI analytics capabilities are more likely to be present; they are also much more likely to be valuable. AI analytics complement certain types of innovation because they enable firms to expand the search space of existing knowledge to combine into new technologies. These capabilities also lend themselves well to incremental process improvements.

There is an important caveat, however: Whether AI helps with innovation depends heavily on the *kind* of innovation a company is attempting. Overall, our investigations suggest that firms that have historically focused on specific types of innovation—process innovation and innovation by diverse recombination, in which companies combine a wide variety of technology elements in new ways—may benefit most from using advanced data capabilities of machine learning and AI. Firms that use AI analytics to generate wide recombinations are 3% to 7% more productive than firms that do not. Furthermore, when a firm's existing knowledge is spread throughout the firm, advanced AI capabilities can further boost firm innovation by about three more new patents a year.

Conversely, using AI is less helpful for incremental innovation and making small improvements to existing products, and is almost no help at all for radical innovation. Not only is it not beneficial, but when firms use data analytics for radical innovation, firm performance may suffer. After all, these radical innovations often require human creativity to interpret small data. For instance, the creator of Artemisinin, the first effective drug to treat malaria, relied on a single line of ancient Chinese text.[11] AI will be of little use in this situation because AI-based techniques require far, far more than a single data point. Worse, using expensive machine learning resources to solve ill-suited problems will ultimately hurt firm profit.

Thus, managers must understand the types of innovation AI can help with and the types it cannot.

How to Apply AI to Innovation Processes

To know how AI can help your company's innovation efforts, leaders should consider a few questions:

- *Are you a fast follower?* Using AI can help improve upon existing products and create new products by recombining elements from prior successes. Advanced data capabilities will likely help, as you can use AI to amplify existing abilities in a new way.

- *Are you struggling with a deluge of data?* While many researchers have deep expertise in one or two areas, emerging data technologies can help find technology elements from wide and distant fields. Broad synthesis is critical for these firms to combine these technologies to solve problems in their own domain.

- *Are you overwhelmed with choices?* To succeed, you need to invest in AI projects that support recombination as well as hire AI talents to assess those suggested combinations. You don't need to retrain or hire scientists with AI skills, but you do need to hire AI talents to support scientific efforts.

- *Do you depend on radical innovation?* Using AI probably won't directly benefit innovation efforts. However, using AI can lead to greater follow-up projects once you've made that radical first step. But beware; others can now quickly build on or combine what you've done. You'll need to safeguard your inventions as these innovations create enormous positive externality for others. One possible way is to build a separate arm in the firm that specializes in using analytics to find new combinations based on the new radical innovation you just uncovered. This way, you can realize that externality yourself.

AI is a promising tool for managers to use in innovation. But tools are just tools. How humans use those tools matters. For innovation, we find greater success in organizations using AI to synthesize, combine, and extend rather than hoping for radical new innovations.

Adapted from hbr.org, July 25, 2024. Reprint H08BAE

8

Why Design Thinking Works

by Jeanne M. Liedtka

O ccasionally, a new way of organizing work leads to extraordinary improvements. Total quality management did that in manufacturing in the 1980s by combining a set of tools—kanban cards, quality circles, and so on— with the insight that people on the shop floor could do much higher-level work than they usually were asked to. That blend of tools and insight, applied to a work process, can be thought of as a *social technology*.

In a recent seven-year study in which I looked in depth at 50 projects from a range of sectors, including business, health care, and social services, I have seen that another social technology, design thinking, has the potential to do for innovation exactly what TQM did for manufacturing: unleash people's full creative energies, win their commitment, and radically improve processes. By now most executives have at least heard about design thinking's tools—ethnographic research, an emphasis on reframing problems and experimentation, the use of diverse teams, and so on—if not tried them. But what people may not understand is the subtler way that design thinking gets around the human biases (for example, rootedness in the status quo) or attachments to specific behavioral norms ("That's how we do things here") that time and again block the exercise of imagination.

In this article I'll explore a variety of human tendencies that get in the way of innovation and describe how design thinking's tools and clear process steps help teams break free of them. Let's begin by looking at what organizations need from innovation—and at why their efforts to obtain it often fall short.

The Challenges of Innovation

To be successful, an innovation process must deliver three things: superior solutions, lower risks and costs of change, and employee buy-in. Over the years businesspeople have developed useful tactics for achieving those outcomes. But when trying to apply them, organizations frequently encounter new obstacles and trade-offs.

Superior solutions

Defining problems in obvious, conventional ways, not surprisingly, often leads to obvious, conventional solutions. *Asking a more interesting question* can help teams discover more-original ideas. The risk is that some teams may get indefinitely hung up exploring a problem, while action-oriented managers may be too impatient to take the time to figure out what question they should be asking.

It's also widely accepted that solutions are much better when they incorporate *user-driven criteria*. Market research can help

Idea in Brief

The Problem

While we know a lot about what practices stimulate new ideas and creative solutions, most innovation teams struggle to realize their benefits.

The Cause

People's intrinsic biases and behavioral habits inhibit the exercise of the imagination and protect unspoken assumptions about what will or will not work.

The Solution

Design thinking provides a structured process that helps innovators break free of counterproductive tendencies that thwart innovation. Like TQM, it is a social technology that blends practical tools with insights into human nature.

companies understand those criteria, but the hurdle here is that it's hard for customers to know they want something that doesn't yet exist.

Finally, bringing *diverse voices* into the process is also known to improve solutions. This can be difficult to manage, however, if conversations among people with opposing views deteriorate into divisive debates.

Lower risks and costs

Uncertainty is unavoidable in innovation. That's why innovators often build a *portfolio of options*. The trade-off is that too many ideas dilute focus and resources. To manage this tension, innovators must be willing to let go of bad ideas—to "call the baby ugly," as a manager in one of my studies described it. Unfortunately, people often find it easier to kill the creative (and arguably riskier) ideas than to kill the incremental ones.

Employee buy-in

An innovation won't succeed unless a company's employees get behind it. The surest route to winning their support is to involve them in the process of generating ideas. The danger is that the involvement of many people with different perspectives will create chaos and incoherence.

Underlying the trade-offs associated with achieving these outcomes is a more fundamental tension. In a stable environment, efficiency is achieved by driving variation out of the organization. But in an unstable world, variation becomes the organization's friend, because it opens new paths to success. However, who can blame leaders who must meet quarterly targets for doubling down on efficiency, rationality, and centralized control?

To manage all the trade-offs, organizations need a social technology that addresses these behavioral obstacles as well as the counterproductive biases of human beings. And as I'll explain next, design thinking fits that bill.

The Beauty of Structure

Experienced designers often complain that design thinking is too structured and linear. And for them, that's certainly true. But managers on innovation teams generally are not designers and also aren't used to doing face-to-face research with customers, getting deeply immersed in their perspectives, cocreating with stakeholders, and designing and executing experiments. Structure and linearity help managers try to adjust to these new behaviors.

As Kaaren Hanson, formerly the head of design innovation at Intuit and now Facebook's design product director, has

Shaping the innovator's journey

What makes design thinking a social technology is its ability to counteract the biases of innovators and change the way they engage in the innovation process.

Problem	Design thinking	Improved outcome
Innovators are:		
Trapped in their own expertise and experience	**Provides immersion** in the user's experience, shifting an innovator's mindset toward . . .	A better understanding of those being designed for
Overwhelmed by the volume and messiness of qualitative data	**Makes sense** of data by organizing it into themes and patterns, pointing the innovator toward . . .	New insights and possibilities
Divided by differences in team members' perspectives	**Builds alignment** as insights are translated into design criteria, moving an innovation team toward . . .	Convergence around what really matters to users
Confronted by too many disparate but familiar ideas	**Encourages the emergence** of fresh ideas through a focused inquiry, shifting team members toward . . .	A limited but diverse set of potential new solutions
Constrained by existing biases about what does or doesn't work	**Fosters articulation** of the conditions necessary to each idea's success and transitions a team toward . . .	Clarity on make-or-break assumptions that enables the design of meaningful experiments
Lacking a shared understanding of new ideas and often unable to get good feedback from users	**Offers pre-experiences** to users through very rough prototypes that help innovators get . . .	Accurate feedback at low cost and an understanding of potential solutions' true value
Afraid of change and ambiguity surrounding the new future	**Delivers learning in action** as experiments engage staff and users, helping them build . . .	A shared commitment and confidence in the new product or strategy

explained: "Anytime you're trying to change people's behavior, you need to start them off with a lot of structure, so they don't have to think. A lot of what we do is habit, and it's hard to change those habits, but having very clear guardrails can help us."

Organized processes keep people on track and curb the tendency to spend too long exploring a problem or to impatiently skip ahead. They also instill confidence. Most humans are driven by a fear of mistakes, so they focus more on preventing errors than on seizing opportunities. They opt for inaction rather than action when a choice risks failure. But there is no innovation without action—so psychological safety is essential. The physical props and highly formatted tools of design thinking deliver that sense of security, helping would-be innovators move more assuredly through the discovery of customer needs, idea generation, and idea testing.

In most organizations the application of design thinking involves seven activities. Each generates a clear output that the next activity converts to another output until the organization arrives at an implementable innovation. But at a deeper level, something else is happening—something that executives generally are not aware of. Though ostensibly geared to understanding and molding the experiences of customers, each design-thinking activity also reshapes the experiences of the *innovators themselves* in profound ways.

Customer Discovery

Many of the best-known methods of the design-thinking discovery process relate to identifying the "job to be done." Adapted from the fields of ethnography and sociology, these methods concentrate on examining what makes for a meaningful customer journey rather than on the collection and analysis of data. This exploration entails three sets of activities:

Immersion

Traditionally, customer research has been an impersonal exercise. An expert, who may well have preexisting theories about customer preferences, reviews feedback from focus groups, surveys, and, if available, data on current behavior, and draws inferences about needs. The better the data, the better the inferences. The trouble is, this grounds people in the already articulated needs that the data reflects. They see the data through the lens of their own biases. And they don't recognize needs people have *not* expressed.

Design thinking takes a different approach: Identify hidden needs by having the innovator live the customer's experience. Consider what happened at the Kingwood Trust, a UK charity helping adults with autism and Asperger's syndrome. One design team member, Katie Gaudion, got to know Pete, a nonverbal adult with autism. The first time she observed him at his home, she saw him engaged in seemingly damaging acts—like picking at a leather sofa and rubbing indents in a wall. She started by documenting Pete's behavior and defined the problem as how to prevent such destructiveness.

But on her second visit to Pete's home, she asked herself: What if Pete's actions were motivated by something other than a destructive impulse? Putting her personal perspective aside, she mirrored his behavior and discovered how satisfying his activities actually felt. "Instead of a ruined sofa, I now perceived Pete's sofa as an object wrapped in fabric that is fun to pick," she explained. "Pressing my ear against the wall and feeling the vibrations of the music above, I felt a slight tickle in my ear whilst rubbing the smooth and beautiful indentation . . . So instead of a damaged wall, I perceived it as a pleasant and relaxing audio-tactile experience."

Katie's immersion in Pete's world not only produced a deeper understanding of his challenges but called into question an unexamined bias about the residents, who had been perceived as disability sufferers that needed to be kept safe. Her experience caused her to ask herself another new question: Instead of designing just for residents' disabilities and safety, how could the innovation team design for their strengths and pleasures? That led to the creation of living spaces, gardens, and new activities aimed at enabling people with autism to live fuller and more pleasurable lives.

Sense making

Immersion in user experiences provides raw material for deeper insights. But finding patterns and making sense of the mass of qualitative data collected is a daunting challenge. Time and again, I have seen initial enthusiasm about the results of ethnographic tools fade as nondesigners become overwhelmed by the volume of information and the messiness of searching for deeper insights. It is here that the structure of design thinking really comes into its own.

One of the most effective ways to make sense of the knowledge generated by immersion is a design-thinking exercise called the Gallery Walk. In it the core innovation team selects the most important data gathered during the discovery process and writes it down on large posters. Often these posters showcase individuals who have been interviewed, complete with their photos and quotations capturing their perspectives. The posters are hung around a room, and key stakeholders are invited to tour this gallery and write down on Post-it notes the bits of data they consider essential to new designs. The stakeholders then form small teams, and in a carefully orchestrated process, their Post-it observations are shared, combined, and sorted by theme into clusters that the group mines for insights. This process overcomes the danger that innovators will be unduly influenced by their own biases and see only what they want to see, because it makes the people who were interviewed feel vivid and real to those browsing the gallery. It creates a common database and facilitates collaborators' ability to interact, reach shared insights together, and challenge one another's individual takeaways—another critical guard against biased interpretations.

Alignment

The final stage in the discovery process is a series of workshops and seminar discussions that ask in some form the question, If anything were possible, what job would the design do well? The focus on possibilities, rather than on the constraints imposed by the status quo, helps diverse teams have more-collaborative and creative discussions about the design criteria, or the set of key features that an ideal innovation should have. Establishing a spirit of inquiry deepens dissatisfaction with the status quo and makes it easier for teams to reach consensus throughout the innovation process. And down the road, when the portfolio of ideas is winnowed, agreement on the design criteria will give novel ideas a fighting chance against safer incremental ones.

Consider what happened at Monash Health, an integrated hospital and health care system in Melbourne, Australia. Mental health clinicians there had long been concerned about the frequency of patient relapses—usually in the form of drug overdoses and suicide attempts—but consensus on how to address this problem eluded them. In an effort to get to the bottom of it, clinicians traced the experiences of specific patients through the treatment process. One patient, Tom, emerged as emblematic in their study. His experience included three face-to-face visits with different clinicians, 70 touchpoints, 13 different case managers, and 18 handoffs during the interval between his initial visit and his relapse.

The team members held a series of workshops in which they asked clinicians this question: Did Tom's current care exemplify why they had entered health care? As people discussed their motivations for becoming doctors and nurses, they came to realize that improving Tom's outcome might depend as much on their sense of duty to Tom himself as it did on their clinical activity. Everyone bought into this conclusion, which made designing a new treatment process—centered on the patient's needs rather than perceived best practices—proceed smoothly and successfully. After its implementation, patient-relapse rates fell by 60%.

Idea Generation

Once they understand customers' needs, innovators move on to identify and winnow down specific solutions that conform to the criteria they've identified.

Emergence

The first step here is to set up a dialogue about potential solutions, carefully planning who will participate, what challenge they will be given, and how the conversation will be structured. After using the design criteria to do some individual brainstorming, participants gather to share ideas and build on them creatively—as opposed to simply negotiating compromises when differences arise.

When Children's Health System of Texas, the sixth-largest pediatric medical center in the United States, identified the need for a new strategy, the organization, led by the vice president of population health, Peter Roberts, applied design thinking to reimagine its business model. During the discovery process, clinicians set aside their bias that what mattered most was medical intervention. They came to understand that intervention alone wouldn't work if the local population in Dallas didn't have the time or ability to seek out medical knowledge and didn't have strong support networks—something few families in the area enjoyed. The clinicians also realized that the medical center couldn't successfully address problems on its own; the community would need to be central to any solution. So Children's Health invited its community partners to codesign a new wellness ecosystem whose boundaries (and resources) would stretch far beyond the medical center. Deciding to start small and tackle a single condition, the team gathered to create a new model for managing asthma.

The session brought together hospital administrators, physicians, nurses, social workers, parents of patients, and staff from Dallas's school districts, housing authority, YMCA, and faith-based organizations. First, the core innovation team shared learning from the discovery process. Next, each attendee thought independently about the capabilities that their institution might contribute toward addressing the children's problems, jotting down ideas on sticky notes. Then each attendee was invited to join a small group at one of five tables, where the participants shared individual ideas, grouped them into common themes, and envisioned what an ideal experience would look like for the young patients and their families.

Champions of change usually emerge from these kinds of conversations, which greatly improves the chances of successful implementation. (All too often, good ideas die on the vine in the absence of people with a personal commitment to making them happen.) At Children's Health, the partners invited into the project galvanized the community to act and forged and maintained the relationships in their institutions required to realize the new vision. Housing authority representatives drove changes in housing codes, charging inspectors with incorporating children's health issues (like the presence of mold) into their assessments. Local pediatricians adopted a set of standard asthma protocols, and parents of children with asthma took on a significant role as peer counselors providing intensive education to other families through home visits.

Articulation

Typically, emergence activities generate a number of competing ideas, more or less attractive and more or less feasible. In the next step, articulation, innovators surface and question their implicit assumptions. Managers are often bad at this, because of many behavioral biases, such as overoptimism, confirmation bias, and fixation on first solutions. When assumptions aren't challenged, discussions around what will or won't work become deadlocked, with each person advocating from their own understanding of how the world works.

In contrast, design thinking frames the discussion as an inquiry into what would have to be true about the world for an idea to be feasible. (See "Management Is Much More Than a Science," by Roger L. Martin and Tony Golsby-Smith, HBR,

September–October 2017.) An example of this comes from the Ignite Accelerator program of the U.S. Department of Health and Human Services. At the Whiteriver Indian reservation hospital in Arizona, a team led by Marliza Rivera, a young quality control officer, sought to reduce wait times in the hospital's emergency room, which were sometimes as long as six hours.

The team's initial concept, borrowed from Johns Hopkins Hospital in Baltimore, was to install an electronic kiosk for check-in. As team members began to apply design thinking, however, they were asked to surface their assumptions about why the idea would work. It was only then that they realized that their patients, many of whom were elderly Apache speakers, were unlikely to be comfortable with computer technology. Approaches that worked in urban Baltimore would not work in Whiteriver, so this idea could be safely set aside.

At the end of the idea generation process, innovators will have a portfolio of well-thought-through, though possibly quite different, ideas. The assumptions underlying them will have been carefully vetted, and the conditions necessary for their success will be achievable. The ideas will also have the support of committed teams, who will be prepared to take on the responsibility of bringing them to market.

The Testing Experience

Companies often regard prototyping as a process of fine-tuning a product or service that has already largely been developed. But in design thinking, prototyping is carried out on far-from-finished products. It's about users' iterative experiences with a work in progress. This means that quite radical changes—including complete redesigns—can occur along the way.

Pre-experience

Neuroscience research indicates that helping people "pre-experience" something novel—or to put it another way, *imagine* it incredibly vividly—results in more-accurate assessments of the novelty's value. That's why design thinking calls for the creation of basic, low-cost artifacts that will capture the essential features of the proposed user experience. These are not literal prototypes—and they are often much rougher than the "minimum viable products" that lean startups test with customers. But what these artifacts lose in fidelity, they gain in flexibility, because they can easily be altered in response to what's learned by exposing users to them. And their incompleteness invites interaction.

Such artifacts can take many forms. The layout of a new medical office building at Kaiser Permanente, for example, was tested by hanging bedsheets from the ceiling to mark future walls. Nurses and physicians were invited to interact with staffers who were playing the role of patients and to suggest how spaces could be adjusted to better facilitate treatment. At Monash Health, a program called Monash Watch—aimed at using telemedicine to keep vulnerable populations healthy at home and reduce their hospitalization rates—used detailed storyboards to help hospital administrators and government policymakers envision this new approach in practice, without building a digital prototype.

Learning in action

Real-world experiments are an essential way to assess new ideas and identify the changes needed to make them workable. But such tests offer another, less obvious kind of value: They help reduce employees' and customers' quite normal fear of change.

Consider an idea proposed by Don Campbell, a professor of medicine, and Keith Stockman, a manager of operations research at Monash Health. As part of Monash Watch, they suggested hiring laypeople to be "telecare" guides who would act as "professional neighbors," keeping in frequent telephone contact with patients at high risk of multiple hospital admissions. Campbell and Stockman hypothesized that lower-wage laypeople who were carefully selected, trained in health literacy and empathy skills, and backed by a decision support system and professional coaches they could involve as needed could help keep the at-risk patients healthy at home.

Their proposal was met with skepticism. Many of their colleagues held a strong bias against letting anyone besides a health professional perform such a service for patients with complex issues, but using health professionals in the role would have been unaffordable. Rather than debating this point, however, the innovation team members acknowledged the concerns and engaged their colleagues in the codesign of an experiment testing that assumption. Three hundred patients later, the results were in: overwhelmingly positive patient feedback and a demonstrated reduction in bed use and emergency room visits, corroborated by independent consultants, quelled the fears of the skeptics.

. . .

As we have seen, the structure of design thinking creates a natural flow from research to rollout. Immersion in the customer experience produces data, which is transformed into insights, which help teams agree on design criteria they use to brainstorm solutions. Assumptions about what's critical to the success of

those solutions are examined and then tested with rough prototypes that help teams further develop innovations and prepare
them for real-world experiments.

Along the way, design-thinking processes counteract human
biases that thwart creativity while addressing the challenges
typically faced in reaching superior solutions, lowered costs
and risks, and employee buy-in. Recognizing organizations as
collections of human beings who are motivated by varying perspectives and emotions, design thinking emphasizes engagement, dialogue, and learning. By involving customers and other
stakeholders in the definition of the problem and the development of solutions, design thinking garners a broad commitment
to change. And by supplying a structure to the innovation process, design thinking helps innovators collaborate and agree
on what is essential to the outcome at every phase. It does this
not only by overcoming workplace politics but by shaping the
experiences of the innovators, and of their key stakeholders and
implementers, at every step. *That* is social technology at work.

Originally published in September–October 2018. Reprint R1805D

If Your Innovation Effort Isn't Working, Look at Who's on the Team

by Nathan Furr, Kyle Nel, and
Thomas Zoëga Ramsøy

An all-star team is making headway with a new initiative that could alter the future of the organization. Spirits are optimistic, and the team is successfully maneuvering through new yet very promising territory. Then, the results begin taking longer than anticipated to prove, and after too much time spent outside their comfort zones, the team of high-achieving employees can't seem to execute within the uncertain environment.

The team's outlook shifts, and it becomes clear that the group will not be able to weather the storm of uncertainty needed to realize this new organizational opportunity.

How could such a capable team fail?

At the heart of many organizations is a deeper problem that blocks transformation: product/function organizational structure. This structure works in well-understood environments, where maximizing delivery of a product or service is the goal, but transformative projects require the organization to return to a more malleable state. This challenge requires teams that are formed by rematching resources and employee capabilities.

Transformation-capable teams are made up of people who not only are high performers but also hold a unique balance of skills and mindsets that allow them to sustain focus, agility, and optimism in the face of uncertainty for prolonged periods of time. Ultimately, not all top-performing employees are equipped for this.

In our book, *Leading Transformation: How to Take Charge of Your Company's Future*, we highlight certain capabilities to search for and cultivate while building a transformative team. Specifically, there are three unique characteristics that will play critical roles as a team takes on a breakthrough initiative.

Negative Capability: Being Comfortable with Uncertainty

The term *negative capability* was coined by the poet John Keats while describing writers like Shakespeare who were able to work within uncertainty and doubt. Negative capability is the ability to accept not having an immediate answer and to remain willing to explore how something may evolve before there is a clear outcome.

In the modern context, negative capability can be thought of as the ability to be comfortable with uncertainty, even to entertain it, rather than to become so anxious by its presence that you have to prematurely race to a more certain yet suboptimal conclusion. Whereas many people cannot stand the fuzziness of

Idea in Brief

The Problem

At the heart of many organizations is a deep problem that blocks transformation: the traditional product/function structure. This structure works in well-understood environments, but transformative projects require the organization to build transformative teams for success.

The Solution

Transformation-capable teams are composed of individuals who not only are high performers but also hold a unique balance of skills and neuropsychological aptitudes that allow them to sustain focus, agility, and optimism as they operate within uncertainty for prolonged periods of time. There are three unique characteristics that are most critical as teams take on breakthrough initiatives: negative capability, chaos pilots, and divergent thinking.

uncertainty, those who demonstrate negative capabilities can facilitate the exploration of new terrain and the discovery of an adjacent possible opportunity.

Individuals with negative capability remain curious and focused even when your project is far from the end goal. Chances are, they will even find this point of the project enthralling, rather than overwhelming, which is exactly what you want. They will also be able to suspend judgment about an end result and stay open to many possible outcomes, rather than become fixed early on to one version of success.

Chaos Pilots: Leading and Executing in Unfamiliar Territory

In 1991 Danish politician and social worker Uffe Elbæk took out a $100,000 personal loan to open an unusual business school called Kaospilot. The vision of the business school was inspired by a previous project of Elbæk's, where he observed a new skill set in students for navigating uncertain problems and saw the opportunity to teach these skills to business leaders who needed to do the same. *Chaos pilot* is a perfect label for a specific persona needed on a transformative team.

Chaos pilots are people who can creatively lead a project through uncertainty. They have negative capability, but they also have other critical skills, such as the ability to create structure within chaos and take action. Leaders who are chaos pilots are able to drive a team forward on a project even as the environment around them fluctuates.

Although it may sound glamorous to be such a person, being a chaos pilot is hard—they are the colleagues working on ambiguous projects and frequently getting beat up in the process. People who aren't capable of being chaos pilots quickly flounder when the environment around the project gets shaky.

Chaos pilots often care more about creating meaningful change than about climbing the corporate ladder or getting another star on their charts. Finding chaos pilots to join you can be challenging and requires observation and experimentation, though there are a few fertile places to search for good candidates.

For example, look for people who are getting mixed performance reviews but are still highly prized by the organization. Often, these people are getting mixed reviews because they make those around them uncomfortable—the potential candidates often challenge the status quo—but they continue to succeed because they perform so well.

Divergent Thinking, Convergent Action, and Influential Communication

Finally, there are three neuropsychological traits to seek while building a transformative team. These three traits—divergent thinking, convergent action, and influential communication—all play a crucial role in succeeding in innovation and transformation. While many individuals hold one or two of these skills, finding a person with all three is more challenging, yet optimal.

The first of the three, divergent thinking, is the ability to uniquely connect new information, ideas, and concepts that are usually held far apart. People with this skill can match dissimilar concepts in novel and meaningful ways and uncover new opportunities that others may have overlooked.

Convergent action, the second trait, is the ability to execute on these new ideas to create something tangible. Though many people can come up with great ideas, it is often those with convergent action who will move that new concept from idea to product.

Last, having the ability to communicate ideas in a coherent, compelling, and influential way is paramount. This trait will inspire other leaders and decision-makers to believe, support, and act on a novel idea or opportunity.

Similar to how many transformative business opportunities are found in unlikely places, the same is true about where you may find the best-suited team members to drive forward a promising new initiative.

Each organizational project represents a moment of potential transformation, and each successful project helps an organization self-correct away from becoming a callous machine executing on routine and instead become what it needs to survive: a malleable organization capable of capturing new opportunities.

Adapted from hbr.org, November 9, 2018. Reprint H04N87

9

What's Your Best Innovation Bet?

by Melissa A. Schilling

W hen companies develop new technologies, they can never be certain how the market will respond. That said, the future of a given technology is not as unforeseeable as it might seem. When I work with tech companies on crafting or refining their innovation strategy, I start with an exercise that helps them anticipate where the next big breakthroughs will—or should—be. Central to the exercise is an examination of the key dimensions on which a technology has evolved—say, processing speed in computing—and the degree to which users' needs have been satisfied. This can give companies insight into where to focus their effort and money while helping them anticipate both the moves of competitors and threats from outsiders.

One of my favorite examples comes from the consumer electronics and recording industries, which competed on the basis of audio fidelity for decades. By the mid-1990s, both industries were eager to introduce a next-generation audio format. In 1996 Toshiba, Hitachi, Time Warner, and others formed a consortium to back a new technology, called DVD-Audio, that offered superior fidelity and surround sound. They hoped to do an end run around Sony and Philips, which owned the compact disc standard and extracted a licensing fee for every CD and player sold.

Sony and Philips, however, were not going to go down without a fight. They counterattacked with a new format they had jointly developed, Super Audio CD. Those in the music industry gave a collective groan; manufacturers, distributors, and consumers all stood to lose big if they bet on the wrong format. Nonetheless, Sony launched the first Super Audio players in late 1999; DVD-Audio players hit the market in mid-2000. A costly format war seemed inevitable.

You may be scratching your head at this point, wondering why you've never heard about this format war. What happened? MP3 happened. While the consumer electronics giants were pursuing new heights in audio fidelity, an algorithm that slightly *depressed* fidelity in exchange for reduced audio file size was taking off. Soon after the file-sharing platform Napster launched in 1999, consumers were downloading free music files by the millions, and Napster-like services were sprouting up like weeds.

You might be inclined to think that Sony, Philips, and the DVD-Audio consortium were just unlucky. After all, who could have predicted the disruptive arrival of MP3? How could the consumer electronics giants have known that a format on a trajectory of ever-increasing fidelity would be overtaken by a technology with *less* fidelity? Actually, with the methodology outlined below, they *could* have foreseen that the next breakthrough would probably not be about better fidelity.

Idea in Brief

The Challenge

Successful technology innovation requires firms to make good predictions about product and service capabilities that consumers will value in the future. Getting this wrong can be costly.

The Solution

By studying how a technology has evolved along key dimensions, and understanding the degree to which consumers' needs have been satisfied on those dimensions, it's possible to determine where best to invest in further technology development.

The Proof

Applying this approach, teams across industries have conceived of promising new products that are now in development or launched, including a financial data mobile app and a noninvasive glucose-monitoring technology.

Understanding what's driving technological developments isn't just for high-tech firms. Technology—the way inputs are transformed into outputs, or the way products and services are delivered to customers—evolves in every market. I have used the three-step exercise described here with managers from a wide range of organizations, including companies developing blood-sugar monitors, grocery store chains, hospitals, a paint-thinner manufacturer, and financial services firms. It often yields an "Aha!" moment that helps managers refine or even redirect their innovation strategy.

Step One: Identify Key Dimensions

It's common to talk about a "technology trajectory," as if innovation advances along a single path. But technologies typically progress along several dimensions at once. For example, computers became faster and smaller in tandem; speed was one dimension, size another. Developments in any dimension come with specific costs and benefits and have measurable and changing utility for customers. Identifying the key dimensions of a technology's progression is the first step in predicting its future.

To determine these dimensions, trace the technology's evolution to date, starting as far back as possible. Consider what need the technology originally fulfilled, and then for each major change in its form and function, think about what fundamental elements were affected.

To illustrate, let's return to music-recording technology. Tracing its history reveals six dimensions that have been central to its development: desynchronization, cost, fidelity, music selection, portability, and customizability. Before the invention of the phonograph, people could hear music or a speech only when and where it was performed. When Thomas Edison and Alexander Graham Bell began working on their phonographs in the late 1800s, their primary objective was to *desynchronize* the time and place of a performance so that it could be heard anytime, anywhere. Edison's device—a rotating cylinder covered in foil—was a remarkable achievement, but it was cumbersome, and making copies was difficult. Bell's wax-covered cardboard cylinders, followed by Emile Berliner's flat, disc-shaped records and, later, the development of magnetic tape, made it significantly easier to mass-produce recordings, lowering their *cost* while increasing the *fidelity* and *selection* of music available.

For decades, however, players were bulky and not particularly portable. It was not until the 1960s that eight-track tape cartridges dramatically increased the *portability* of recorded music, as players became common in automobiles. Cassette tapes rose to dominance in the 1970s, further enhancing portability but also offering, for the first time, *customizability*—the ability to create personalized playlists. Then, in 1982, Sony and Philips introduced the compact disc standard, which offered greater fidelity than cassette tapes and rapidly became the dominant format.

When I guide executive teams through step one of the exercise, I emphasize the need to zero in on the *high-level* dimensions along which a technology has evolved—those that are broad enough to encompass other, narrower dimensions. This helps teams see the big picture and avoid getting sidetracked by its details. In audio technology, for example, *recordability* is a specific form of customizability; identifying customizability, rather than the narrower recordability, as a high-level dimension invites exploration of other ways people might want to customize their music experience. For example, they might value a technology that automatically generates a playlist of songs with common characteristics—and indeed, services like Pandora and Spotify emerged to do just that.

It's important to identify dimensions at the optimal "altitude"—neither so low or narrow that they miss the big picture, nor so high or broad that they won't offer adequately detailed insight about a specific technology. In the case of automobiles, for example, climate control may be a technology dimension, but it's so narrow that it's not the most useful one to study; examining the higher-level "comfort" dimension under which it falls will be more illuminating. By the same token, the sweeping "performance" dimension in automobiles is probably too broad a choice, because it includes speed, safety, fuel efficiency, and other dimensions where meaningful advances could be made. Even a product as simple as a mattress involves technology with multiple performance dimensions—such as comfort and durability—that are useful to consider separately.

Selecting dimensions to examine isn't a strict science; it depends substantially on knowledge of your industry—and common sense. I usually ask teams to agree on three to six key dimensions for their technology. The exhibit "A sampling of high-level technology dimensions" lists those identified by workshop participants for their respective industries. Notably, some dimensions, such as ease of use and durability, come up frequently. Others are more specific to a particular technology, such as magnification in microscopes. And with rare exceptions, cost is an important dimension across all technologies.

A final step in this part of the exercise can add further insight about the identified dimensions and in some cases suggest future dimensions worth exploring. I ask team members to disregard cost and other constraints and imagine what customers would want if they could have *anything.* This sounds like it might unleash a flood of creative but impractical ideas. In fact, it can be highly revealing. Folklore has it that Henry Ford once said,

---

A sampling of high-level technology dimensions

Industry professionals can generally agree on three to six dimensions that significantly drive development of their technology.

Technology	Dimensions
Audio	Desynchronization, fidelity, music selection, portability, customizability, cost
Lighting	Durability, brightness, comfort, design selection, cost
Microscopes	Magnification, ease of use, versatility, cost
Painkillers	Strength, reliability, safety, convenience, cost
Transport	Speed, comfort, safety, reliability, ease of use, fuel efficiency, cost

"If I had asked people what they wanted, they would have said faster horses." If any carmaker at the time had really probed people about exactly what their dream conveyance would provide, they probably would have said "instantaneous transportation." Both consumer responses highlight that speed is a high-level dimension valued in transportation, but the latter helps us think more broadly about how it can be achieved. There are only limited ways to make horses go faster—but there are many ways to speed up transportation.

Most of the time this exercise indicates that people want further improvements in the key dimensions already identified. Sometimes, however, the exercise suggests dimensions that have not been considered. Would consumers want an audio device that could sense and respond to their affect? If so, perhaps "anticipation of needs" is another key dimension.

Step Two: Locate Your Position

For each dimension, you next want to determine the shape of its utility curve—the plot of the value consumers derive from a technology according to its performance—and establish where on the curve the technology currently sits. This will help reveal where the greatest opportunity for improvement lies.

For example, the history of audio formats suggests that the selection of music available has a concave parabolic utility curve: Utility increases as selection expands, but at a decreasing rate, and not indefinitely. When there's little music to choose from, even a small increase in selection significantly enhances utility. Consider that when the first phonographs appeared, there were few recordings to play on them. As more became available, customers eagerly bought them, and the appeal of owning a player grew. Increasing selection even a little had a powerful impact on utility. Over the ensuing decades, selection grew exponentially, and the utility curve ultimately began to flatten; people still valued new releases, but each new recording added less additional value. Today digital music services like iTunes, Amazon Prime Music, and Spotify offer tens of millions of songs. With this virtually unlimited selection, most customers' appetites are sated—and we are probably approaching the top of the curve.

Now let's consider the fidelity dimension, the primary focus of Super Audio CD and DVD-Audio. It's likely that fidelity also has a concave parabolic utility curve. The first phonographs had awful fidelity: Music sounded thin and tinny, though it

---

More music, more value—up to a point

For some technologies, small improvements can have a big impact at first. In the early days of recorded music, listeners had few pieces to choose from, so the utility of increasing the selection even a small amount was high. Today consumers have virtually unlimited choices, so the additional utility of increasing selection is low.

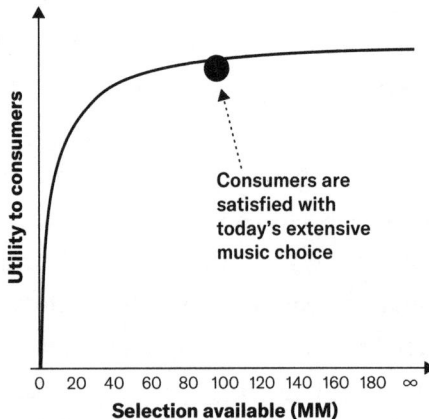

Consumers are satisfied with today's extensive music choice

was still a remarkable benefit to be able to hear any recorded music at all. The early improvements in fidelity that records offered made a big difference in people's enjoyment of music, and sales took off. Then along came compact discs. The higher fidelity they offered was not as widely appreciated—many people felt that vinyl records were good enough, and some even preferred their "warmth." For most consumers, further improvements in fidelity provided little additional utility. The fidelity curve was already leveling out when Sony, Philips, and the DVD-Audio consortium introduced their new formats in the early 2000s.

Both formats offered higher fidelity, by certain technical measures, than the compact disc. For example, whereas CDs have a frequency range up to about 20,000 cycles per second, or 20 kHz, the new formats offered ranges that reached 50 kHz. That's an impressive high end—but because human hearing peaks out at about 20 kHz, only the family dog was likely to appreciate it. In 2007 the Audio Engineering Society released the results of a yearlong trial assessing how well subjects (including professional recording engineers) could detect the difference between Super Audio and regular CDs. Subjects correctly identified the Super Audio CD format only half the time—no better than if they'd been simply guessing.

Had the companies introducing the new formats created even a back-of-the-envelope utility curve for fidelity, they could have seen that there was little room for improvement that customers would appreciate. Meanwhile, even a cursory look at the portability curve would have suggested opportunity on that dimension. Sony, of all companies, should have recognized the importance of portability in the evolution of audio formats. Back in 1979, the company had introduced one of the most successful consumer electronics products ever created—the Sony Walkman. The device, a lightweight cassette player that could fit in one hand, was a runaway hit not because it cost less or offered greater fidelity or selection than other formats but because it was *portable*. Similarly, MP3 was successful because it made music *much more* portable; MP3 files were small enough to be easily stored on a computer and shared with friends.

Fast-forward to today. Although music lovers now take portability and selection for granted, there's still lots of room for improvement on the customizability dimension. Pandora offers primitive customizability (you can create a channel where all the songs sound more or less like Taylor Swift), but artificial intelligence may get us much further up that utility curve in the future. It's plausible (likely, in fact) that a program could identify elements of your preferred music style and then create music for you. Perhaps it would produce an endless stream of "Beatles songs," nearly indistinguishable from the real thing but not written or played by the Beatles (or by any human performer). Machine-learning programs already compose music for advertisements and video games, and in 2016 Sony released two songs composed by an artificial intelligence system called Flow Machines. The first, "Daddy's Car," is reminiscent of the Beatles, and the second, "Mr Shadow," emulates the styles of Duke Ellington, Irving Berlin, and Cole Porter.[1] While neither quite hits the mark, both suggest what's to come—and where music companies might sensibly invest.

Parabolic utility curves like those for audio fidelity and selection show that for some technology performance dimensions, small improvements can have a dramatic impact on utility from the start. Of course, not all technologies follow such utility curves.

High demand for drugs that work

For some technologies, consumers prize even modest advances. Only one of the approved treatments for the neurodegenerative disease ALS extends life span—and only by a few months. Patient demand for effective drugs won't be satisfied until efficacy is 100%, but any improvement up to that point has high utility.

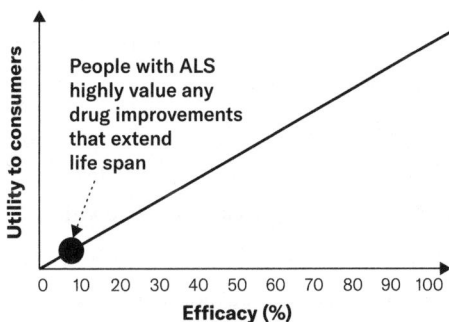

Many dimensions have S-shaped curves: Below some threshold of performance there is no utility, but utility increases quickly above that threshold and then maxes out somewhere beyond that. Consider the utility of a car's speed for an average customer. The first motor vehicles, such as Richard Trevithick's 1801 Puffing Devil, were steam-powered.[2] They offered a proof of concept and were sometimes purchased by wealthy technophiles, but they were too slow and unreliable to be worth the cost to the average family. Horses traveled farther and faster and rarely broke down.

For the next hundred years, inventors sought to develop an automobile that was more useful than a horse-drawn wagon. During this time, the utility curve for speed remained flat; increasing a car's top speed by a few miles an hour offered no additional utility if the car was still slower than a horse— particularly if it was also less reliable, as was typically the case.

It wasn't until the early 20th century, when passenger automobiles started to routinely offer speeds over 15 miles per hour, that they began to be adopted in serious numbers. By the 1990s most passenger cars had a top speed of about 120 mph, and today for many it's near 150 mph. It's uncommon, however, for drivers to exceed 90 mph; for most drivers, the utility curve for speed flattens out at that point. Improvements in other dimensions, such as fuel efficiency, acceleration, safety, and reliability, offer more utility to most customers.

The utility curve for speed reveals that the point at which improvements in a dimension are of little value can change with shifts in the environment or in enabling technologies. Forty miles per hour probably seemed more than fast enough, for example, when the Model T was introduced, since most roads at the time weren't paved. As roads improved and highways appeared, the top speeds desired by customers shifted upward.

The car-speed sweet spot

Some technology improvements have little appeal early on and then quickly grow in value before their utility levels off. The first cars were too slow to be very useful. As they became faster and roads improved, consumers valued ever-greater top speeds—up to about 90 miles per hour. Beyond that, extra speed makes no difference to most drivers.

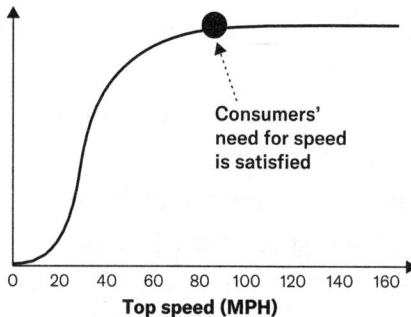

Consumers'
need for speed
is satisfied

0   20   40   60   80   100   120   140   160
Top speed (MPH)

The move to autonomous vehicles may make even higher speeds safe, comfortable, and desirable. If so, the flat top of the current utility curve for speed may slope upward once again.

Step Three: Determine Your Focus

Once you know the dimensions along which your firm's technology has (or can be) improved and where you are on the utility curves for those dimensions, it should be straightforward to identify where the most room for improvement exists. But it's not enough to know that performance on a given dimension *can* be enhanced; you need to decide whether it *should* be. So first assess which of the dimensions you've identified are most important to customers. Then assess the cost and difficulty of addressing each dimension.

For example, of the four dimensions that have been central to automobile development—speed, cost, comfort, and safety—which do customers value most, and which are easiest or most cost-effective to address? On the speed dimension, cars are already at the top of the utility curve, and top speed is relatively difficult and expensive to increase: Higher speed requires more power, which requires a bigger engine, which reduces fuel efficiency and increases cost. Comfort is probably the easiest dimension to address, but is it as important to consumers as safety? And how much does it cost to improve performance on these dimensions?

Tata Motors' experience with the Nano is instructive. The Nano was designed as an affordable car for drivers in India, so it needed to be cheap enough to compete with two-wheeled scooters. The manufacturer cut costs in several ways: The Nano had only a two-cylinder engine and few amenities—no radio, electric

How to improve glucose monitoring?

To prioritize their innovation efforts, the makers of a blood-sugar monitoring device listed the technology dimensions they knew customers cared about most and scored each one according to how important it was, how much improvement was possible, and how easily improvements could be made. The high total score for comfort led the company to develop a noninvasive device.

Dimension	Importance to customers (1–5 scale)	Room for improvement (1–5 scale)	Ease of improvement (1–5 scale)	Total score
Reliability	5	1	1	7
Comfort	4	4	3	**11**
Cost	4	2	2	8
Ease of use	3	2	3	8

windows or locks, antilock brakes, power steering, or airbags. Its seats had a simple three-position recline, the windshield had a single wiper, and there was only one rearview mirror. In 2014, after the Nano received zero stars for safety in crash tests, analysts pointed out that adding airbags and making simple adjustments to the frame could significantly improve the car's safety for less than $100 per vehicle. Tata took this under advisement—and placed its bets on comfort. All 2017 models include air-conditioning and power steering but not airbags.

To assess which technology investments are likely to yield the biggest bang for the buck, managers can use a matrix like the one in the exhibit "How to improve glucose monitoring?" First, for the technology being examined, list the performance dimensions you've identified as most important. (For cars, for example, that might be cost, safety, and comfort.) Then score each dimension on a scale of 1 to 5 in three areas:

- *Importance to customers* (1 = "not important" and 5 = "very important")

- *Room for improvement* (1 = "minor opportunity" and 5 = "major opportunity")

- *Ease of improvement* (1 = "very difficult" and 5 = "very easy")

The exhibit shows a manufacturer's scores on four dimensions of blood-glucose monitors: reliability, comfort, cost, and ease of use. The team identified reliability as most important to customers; having accurate glucose measures can be a matter of life and death. However, existing devices (most of which require a finger prick) are already very reliable and thus scored low on the "room for improvement" measure. They are also fairly easy to use and reasonably low in cost—but they are uncomfortable. Comfort is highly valued yet has much room for improvement. Both comfort and ease of use are moderately difficult to improve (scoring 3s), but because comfort is more important to customers and has more room for improvement, this dimension received the higher total score. So comfort became the focus for innovation efforts; the company began to develop a patch worn on the skin that would detect glucose levels from sweat and would send readings via Bluetooth to the user's smartphone.

Notably, with a simple manipulation, the weight of the matrix scores can be adjusted to reflect any organization's particular situation. For example, if a company is cash-strapped or under other duress, it may want to prioritize easy-to-improve dimensions rather than pursue those that have the greatest potential but are harder to address. If the scale for ease of improvement is switched to 1–10 (while the other scales are kept at 1–5), ease-of-improvement scores can be expected to roughly double and thus have a greater influence on total scores. Alternatively, a company seeking breakthrough innovation might extend the scale for importance to customers, the scale for room for improvement, or both.

From exercise to innovation

By examining the evolution of key technology dimensions, teams across industries have conceived and launched an array of promising new products.

Technology area	Key technology dimensions	Resulting product concept (dimension selected for development)	Status
Glucose monitoring	Reliability, comfort, ease of use, cost	Noninvasive glucose-monitoring skin patch streams data to mobile device. (COMFORT, EASE OF USE)	In development by industry and university teams
Sports television	Selection, social interactivity, immersiveness, cost	Virtual reality platform allows separated viewers to watch games in a shared virtual space. (SOCIAL INTERACTIVITY, IMMERSIVENESS)	2017 launch expected
Financial data	Speed, accuracy, breadth, usability, portability, cost	Mobile app provides instant access to proprietary high-value content and analytics. (USABILITY, PORTABILITY)	App released in 2013 is now among the top three in financial services
Academic publishing	Reach, access, impact, searchability, cost	Online portal enhances research discoverability and collaboration. (IMPACT, SEARCHABILITY)	Launched in early 2017

Similarly, a company's competitive positioning may affect which technology dimensions it emphasizes. For example, safety may be a key differentiator for an automaker such as Volvo, while speed (or, more broadly, driving performance) may be the differentiator for BMW. So although the companies make

Getting an Edge on Competitors

The technology assessment exercise can help companies anticipate competitors' moves. Because competitors may differ in their
capabilities (making particular technology dimensions harder or
easier for them to address), or because they may focus on different
segments (influencing which dimensions seem most important or
have the most room for improvement), they are likely to come up
with different rankings for a given set of dimensions.

For example, managers at a financial technology company
realized that for some of their product offerings, Google could
be considered a potential competitor. The company had identified speed, accuracy, breadth, usability, and portability as key
financial-data dimensions. By considering how Google might
rank those dimensions—probably giving greatest weight to speed
and breadth (areas where it had particular strength)—the firm
determined that Google would be likely to continue directing its
focus there. The firm also realized that usability was an important
differentiator and a dimension where it had a significant advantage over potential competitors. Whereas Google and others could
provide large amounts of searchable, nonproprietary data, the
financial technology company was better positioned to provide
proprietary algorithms that would transform data into meaningful metrics and graphs. With this understanding, the managers
decided to emphasize proprietary analytics in their mobile offering, rather than data feeds alone.

the same technology (cars), they market to different customer
segments and thus emphasize different dimensions.

Shifting the Focus

The three-part exercise I recommend can help managers
broaden their perspective on their industry and shift their focus
from "This is what we do" to "This is where our market is (or

should be) heading." It can also help overcome the bias and inertia that tend to keep an organization's attention locked on technology dimensions that are less important to consumers than they once were. For example, at a large financial services firm I worked with, data-transfer speed had long been a key dimension where the leadership expected to see regular improvements. At its founding, the firm had developed technology to deliver financial data more rapidly than anyone else could. Being faster than competitors was, and remained, central to the company's strategy and a matter of organizational pride. However, when I used this exercise with the firm's managers, they realized that concentrating on data-transfer speed (which was now in the nanoseconds) was diverting their attention away from technology dimensions where there was greater opportunity to make improvements that customers would actually value.

For this firm, data-transfer speed had become what fidelity was to Super Audio CD: It could be improved upon year after year, but it offered diminishing utility to users. Furthermore, speed no longer provided a competitive advantage; technology to move data quickly had become ubiquitous and commoditized. The firm's proprietary algorithms for transforming raw data into strategically useful information were far more defensible. The exercise revealed much greater opportunity for delivering this information on demand. Following the workshop, a group of managers made plans to shift resources into ensuring that their most highly used and differentiated analytics-based products could be effectively delivered on phones and tablets. The result was an award-winning mobile application that is now among the top three financial-services applications worldwide.

Conclusion

New product ideas are not the only—or even the most important—outcome of this exercise. Perhaps more valuable is the big-picture perspective it can give managers—shedding new light on market dynamics and the larger-scale or longer-term opportunities before them. Only then will they be able to lead innovation in their industries rather than scramble to respond to it.

Originally published in July–August 2017. Reprint R1704F

Strategies for Learning from Failure

by Amy C. Edmondson

The wisdom of learning from failure is incontrovertible. Yet organizations that do it well are extraordinarily rare. This gap is not due to a lack of commitment to learning. Managers in the vast majority of enterprises that I have studied over the past 20 years—pharmaceutical, financial services, product design, telecommunications, and construction companies; hospitals; and NASA's space shuttle program, among others—genuinely wanted to help their organizations learn from failures to improve future performance. In some cases they and their teams had devoted many hours to after-action reviews, postmortems, and the like. But time after time I saw that these painstaking efforts led to no real change. The reason: those managers were thinking about failure the wrong way.

Most executives I've talked to believe that failure is bad (of course!). They also believe that learning from it is pretty straightforward: ask people to reflect on what they did wrong and exhort them to avoid similar mistakes in the future—or, better yet, assign a team to review and write a report on what happened and then distribute it throughout the organization.

These widely held beliefs are misguided. First, failure is not always bad. In organizational life it is sometimes bad, sometimes inevitable, and sometimes even good. Second, learning from organizational failures is anything but straightforward. The attitudes and activities required to effectively detect and analyze failures are in short supply in most companies, and the need for context-specific learning strategies is underappreciated. Organizations need new and better ways to go beyond lessons that are superficial ("Procedures weren't followed") or self-serving ("The market just wasn't ready for our great new product"). That means jettisoning old cultural beliefs and stereotypical notions of success and embracing failure's lessons. Leaders can begin by understanding how the blame game gets in the way.

The Blame Game

Failure and fault are virtually inseparable in most households, organizations, and cultures. Every child learns at some point that admitting failure means taking the blame. That is why so few organizations have shifted to a culture of psychological safety in which the rewards of learning from failure can be fully realized.

Executives I've interviewed in organizations as different as hospitals and investment banks admit to being torn: How can they respond constructively to failures without giving rise to an anything-goes attitude? If people aren't blamed for failures, what will ensure that they try as hard as possible to do their best work?

Idea in Brief

The ingrained attitude that all failures are bad means organizations don't learn from them.

Leaders need to recognize that failures occur on a spectrum from blameworthy to praiseworthy, and that they fall into three categories:

- Failures in routine or predictable operations, which can be prevented
- Those in complex operations, which can't be avoided but can be managed so that they don't mushroom into catastrophes
- Unwanted outcomes in, for example, research settings, which are valuable because they generate knowledge

Although learning from failures requires different strategies in different work settings, the goal should be to detect them early, analyze them deeply, and design experiments or pilot projects to produce them. But if the organization is ultimately to succeed, employees must feel safe admitting to and reporting failures. Creating that environment takes strong leadership.

This concern is based on a false dichotomy. In actuality, a culture that makes it safe to admit and report on failure can—and in some organizational contexts *must*—coexist with high standards for performance. To understand why, look at the sidebar "A Spectrum of Reasons for Failure," which lists causes ranging from deliberate deviation to thoughtful experimentation.

Which of these causes involve blameworthy actions? Deliberate deviance, first on the list, obviously warrants blame. But inattention might not. If it results from a lack of effort, perhaps it's blameworthy. But if it results from fatigue near the end of an overly long shift, the manager who assigned the shift is more at fault than the employee. As we go down the list, it gets more and more difficult to find blameworthy acts. In fact, a failure resulting from thoughtful experimentation that generates valuable information may actually be praiseworthy.

When I ask executives to consider this spectrum and then to estimate how many of the failures in their organizations are truly blameworthy, their answers are usually in single digits— perhaps 2% to 5%. But when I ask how many are *treated* as blameworthy, they say (after a pause or a laugh) 70% to 90%. The unfortunate consequence is that many failures go unreported and their lessons are lost.

Not All Failures Are Created Equal

A sophisticated understanding of failure's causes and contexts will help to avoid the blame game and institute an effective strategy for learning from failure. Although an infinite number of things can go wrong in organizations, mistakes fall into three broad categories: preventable, complexity-related, and intelligent.

Preventable failures in predictable operations

Most failures in this category can indeed be considered "bad." They usually involve deviations from spec in the closely defined processes of high-volume or routine operations in manufacturing and services. With proper training and support, employees can follow those processes consistently. When they don't, deviance, inattention, or lack of ability is usually the reason. But in such cases, the causes can be readily identified and solutions developed. Checklists (as in the Harvard surgeon Atul Gawande's recent bestseller *The Checklist Manifesto*) are one solution. Another is the vaunted Toyota Production System, which builds continual learning from tiny failures (small process deviations) into its approach to improvement. As most students of operations know well, a team member on a Toyota assembly line who

A Spectrum of Reasons for Failure

- *Deviance.* An individual chooses to violate a prescribed process or practice.

- *Inattention.* An individual inadvertently deviates from specifications.

- *Lack of ability.* An individual doesn't have the skills, conditions, or training to execute a job.

- *Process inadequacy.* A competent individual adheres to a prescribed but faulty or incomplete process.

- *Task challenge.* An individual faces a task too difficult to be executed reliably every time.

- *Process complexity.* A process composed of many elements breaks down when it encounters novel interactions.

- *Uncertainty.* A lack of clarity about future events causes people to take seemingly reasonable actions that produce undesired results.

- *Hypothesis testing.* An experiment conducted to prove that an idea or a design will succeed fails.

- *Exploratory testing.* An experiment conducted to expand knowledge and investigate a possibility leads to an undesired result.

spots a problem or even a potential problem is encouraged to pull a rope called the andon cord, which immediately initiates a diagnostic and problem-solving process. Production continues unimpeded if the problem can be remedied in less than a minute. Otherwise, production is halted—despite the loss of revenue entailed—until the failure is understood and resolved.

Unavoidable failures in complex systems

A large number of organizational failures are due to the inherent uncertainty of work: A particular combination of needs, people, and problems may have never occurred before. Triaging patients in a hospital emergency room, responding to enemy actions on the battlefield, and running a fast-growing startup all occur in unpredictable situations. And in complex organizations like aircraft carriers and nuclear power plants, system failure is a perpetual risk.

Although serious failures can be averted by following best practices for safety and risk management, including a thorough analysis of any such events that do occur, small process failures are inevitable. To consider them bad is not just a misunderstanding of how complex systems work; it is counterproductive. Avoiding consequential failures means rapidly identifying and correcting small failures. Most accidents in hospitals result from a series of small failures that went unnoticed and unfortunately lined up in just the wrong way.

Intelligent failures at the frontier

Failures in this category can rightly be considered "good," because they provide valuable new knowledge that can help an organization leap ahead of the competition and ensure its future growth—which is why the Duke University professor of management Sim Sitkin calls them intelligent failures. They occur when experimentation is necessary: when answers are not knowable in advance because this exact situation hasn't been encountered before and perhaps never will be again. Discovering new drugs, creating a radically new business, designing an innovative product, and testing customer reactions in a brand-new market are tasks that require intelligent failures. "Trial and error" is a common term for the kind of experimentation needed in these settings, but it is a misnomer, because "error" implies that there was a "right" outcome in the first place. At the frontier, the right kind of experimentation produces good failures quickly. Managers who practice it can avoid the *unintelligent* failure of conducting experiments at a larger scale than necessary.

Leaders of the product design firm IDEO understood this when they launched a new innovation-strategy service. Rather than help clients design new products within their existing lines—a process IDEO had all but perfected—the service would help them create new lines that would take them in novel strategic directions. Knowing that it hadn't yet figured out how to deliver the service effectively, the company started a small project with a mattress company and didn't publicly announce the launch of a new business.

Although the project failed—the client did not change its product strategy—IDEO learned from it and figured out what had to be done differently. For instance, it hired team members with MBAs who could better help clients create new businesses and made some of the clients' managers part of the team. Today strategic innovation services account for more than a third of IDEO's revenues.

Tolerating unavoidable process failures in complex systems and intelligent failures at the frontiers of knowledge won't promote mediocrity. Indeed, tolerance is essential for any organization that wishes to extract the knowledge such failures provide. But failure is still inherently emotionally charged; getting an organization to accept it takes leadership.

Building a Learning Culture

Only leaders can create and reinforce a culture that counteracts the blame game and makes people feel both comfortable with and responsible for surfacing and learning from failures. (See the sidebar "How Leaders Can Build a Psychologically Safe Environment.") They should insist that their organizations develop a clear understanding of what happened—not of "who did it"—when things go wrong. This requires consistently reporting failures, small and large; systematically analyzing them; and proactively searching for opportunities to experiment.

Leaders should also send the right message about the nature of the work, such as reminding people in R&D, "We're in the discovery business, and the faster we fail, the faster we'll succeed." I have found that managers often don't understand or appreciate this subtle but crucial point. They also may approach failure in a way that is inappropriate for the context. For example, statistical process control, which uses data analysis to assess unwarranted variances, is not good for catching and correcting random invisible glitches such as software bugs. Nor does it help in the development of creative new products. Conversely, though great scientists intuitively adhere to IDEO's slogan, "Fail often in order to succeed sooner," it would hardly promote success in a manufacturing plant.

Often one context or one kind of work dominates the culture of an enterprise and shapes how it treats failure. For instance, automotive companies, with their predictable, high-volume operations, understandably tend to view failure as something that can and should be prevented. But most organizations engage in all three kinds of work discussed above—routine, complex, and frontier. Leaders must ensure that the right approach to learning from failure is applied in each. All organizations learn from failure through three essential activities: detection, analysis, and experimentation.

Detecting Failure

Spotting big, painful, expensive failures is easy. But in many organizations any failure that can be hidden *is* hidden as long as it's unlikely to cause immediate or obvious harm. The goal should be to surface it early, before it has mushroomed into disaster.

Shortly after arriving from Boeing to take the reins at Ford, in September 2006, Alan Mulally instituted a new system for detecting failures. He asked managers to color code their reports green for good, yellow for caution, or red for problems—a common management technique. According to a 2009 story in *Fortune*, at his first few meetings all the managers coded their operations green, to Mulally's frustration. Reminding them that the company had lost several billion dollars the previous year, he asked straight out, "Isn't anything *not* going well?" After one tentative yellow report was made about a serious product defect that would probably delay a launch, Mulally responded to the deathly silence that ensued with applause. After that, the weekly staff meetings were full of color.

That story illustrates a pervasive and fundamental problem: Although many methods of surfacing current and pending failures exist, they are grossly underutilized. Total Quality Management and soliciting feedback from customers are well-known techniques for bringing to light failures in routine operations. High-reliability-organization (HRO) practices help prevent catastrophic failures in complex systems like nuclear power plants

How Leaders Can Build a Psychologically Safe Environment

If an organization's employees are to help spot existing and pending failures and to learn from them, their leaders must make it safe to speak up. Julie Morath, the chief operating officer of Children's Hospital and Clinics of Minnesota from 1999 to 2009, did just that when she led a highly successful effort to reduce medical errors. Here are five practices I've identified in my research, with examples of how Morath employed them to build a psychologically safe environment.

Frame the Work Accurately

People need a shared understanding of the kinds of failures that can be expected to occur in a given work context (routine production, complex operations, or innovation) and why openness and collaboration are important for surfacing and learning from them. Accurate framing detoxifies failure.

In a complex operation like a hospital, many consequential failures are the result of a series of small events. To heighten awareness of this system complexity, Morath presented data on U.S. medical error rates, organized discussion groups, and built a team of key influencers from throughout the organization to help spread knowledge and understanding of the challenge.

Embrace Messengers

Those who come forward with bad news, questions, concerns, or mistakes should be rewarded rather than shot. Celebrate the value of the news first and then figure out how to fix the failure and learn from it.

Morath implemented "Blameless Reporting"—an approach that encouraged employees to reveal medical errors and near misses anonymously. Her team created a new patient safety report, which expanded on the previous version by asking employees to describe incidents in their own words and to comment on the possible causes. Soon after the new system was implemented, the rate of reported failures shot up. Morath encouraged her people to view the data as good news, because the hospital could learn from failures—and made sure that teams were assigned to analyze every incident.

Acknowledge Limits

Being open about what you don't know, mistakes you've made, and what you can't get done alone will encourage others to do the same.

As soon as she joined the hospital, Morath explained her passion for patient safety and acknowledged that as a newcomer, she had only limited knowledge of how things worked at Children's. In group presentations and one-on-one discussions, she made clear that she would need everyone's help to reduce errors.

Invite Participation

Ask for observations and ideas and create opportunities for people to detect and analyze failures and promote intelligent experiments. Inviting participation helps defuse resistance and defensiveness.

Morath set up cross-disciplinary teams to analyze failures and personally asked thoughtful questions of employees at all levels. Early on, she invited people to reflect on their recent experiences in caring for patients: Was everything as safe as they would have wanted it to be? This helped them recognize that the hospital had room for improvement. Suddenly, people were lining up to help.

Set Boundaries and Hold People Accountable

Paradoxically, people feel psychologically safer when leaders are clear about what acts are blameworthy. And there must be consequences. But if someone is punished or fired, tell those directly and indirectly affected what happened and why it warranted blame.

When she instituted blameless reporting, Morath explained to employees that although reporting would not be punished, specific behaviors (such as reckless conduct, conscious violation of standards, or failing to ask for help when over one's head) would. If someone makes the same mistake three times and is then laid off, coworkers usually express relief, along with sadness and concern—they understand that patients were at risk and that extra vigilance was required from others to counterbalance the person's shortcomings.

through early detection. Électricité de France, which operates 58 nuclear power plants, has been an exemplar in this area: it goes beyond regulatory requirements and religiously tracks each plant for anything even slightly out of the ordinary, immediately investigates whatever turns up, and informs all its other plants of any anomalies.

Such methods are not more widely employed because all too many messengers—even the most senior executives—remain reluctant to convey bad news to bosses and colleagues. One senior executive I know in a large consumer products company had grave reservations about a takeover that was already in the works when he joined the management team. But, overly conscious of his newcomer status, he was silent during discussions in which all the other executives seemed enthusiastic about the plan. Many months later, when the takeover had clearly failed, the team gathered to review what had happened. Aided by a consultant, each executive considered what they might have done to contribute to the failure. The newcomer, openly apologetic about his past silence, explained that others' enthusiasm had made him unwilling to be "the skunk at the picnic."

In researching errors and other failures in hospitals, I discovered substantial differences across patient-care units in nurses' willingness to speak up about them. It turned out that the behavior of mid-level managers—how they responded to failures and whether they encouraged open discussion of them, welcomed questions, and displayed humility and curiosity—was the cause. I have seen the same pattern in a wide range of organizations.

A horrific case in point, which I studied for more than two years, is the 2003 explosion of the *Columbia* space shuttle, which killed seven astronauts (see "Facing Ambiguous Threats," by Michael A. Roberto, Richard M. J. Bohmer, and

Amy C. Edmondson, HBR, November 2006). NASA managers spent some two weeks downplaying the seriousness of a piece of foam's having broken off the left side of the shuttle at launch. They rejected engineers' requests to resolve the ambiguity (which could have been done by having a satellite photograph the shuttle or asking the astronauts to conduct a space walk to inspect the area in question), and the major failure went largely undetected until its fatal consequences 16 days later. Ironically, a shared but unsubstantiated belief among program managers that there was little they could do contributed to their inability to detect the failure. Postevent analyses suggested that they might indeed have taken fruitful action. But clearly leaders hadn't established the necessary culture, systems, and procedures.

One challenge is teaching people in an organization when to declare defeat in an experimental course of action. The human tendency to hope for the best and try to avoid failure at all costs gets in the way, and organizational hierarchies exacerbate it. As a result, failing R&D projects are often kept going much longer than is scientifically rational or economically prudent. We throw good money after bad, praying that we'll pull a rabbit out of a hat. Intuition may tell engineers or scientists that a project has fatal flaws, but the formal decision to call it a failure may be delayed for months.

Again, the remedy—which does not necessarily involve much time and expense—is to reduce the stigma of failure. Eli Lilly has done this since the early 1990s by holding "failure parties" to honor intelligent, high-quality scientific experiments that fail to achieve the desired results. The parties don't cost much, and redeploying valuable resources—particularly scientists—to new projects earlier rather than later can save hundreds of thousands of dollars, not to mention kick-start potential new discoveries.

Analyzing Failure

Once a failure has been detected, it's essential to go beyond the obvious and superficial reasons for it to understand the root causes. This requires the discipline—better yet, the enthusiasm—to use sophisticated analysis to ensure that the right lessons are learned and the right remedies are employed. The job of leaders is to see that their organizations don't just move on after a failure but stop to dig in and discover the wisdom contained in it.

Why is failure analysis often shortchanged? Because examining our failures in depth is emotionally unpleasant and can chip away at our self-esteem. Left to our own devices, most of us will speed through or avoid failure analysis altogether. Another reason is that analyzing organizational failures requires inquiry and openness, patience, and a tolerance for causal ambiguity. Yet managers typically admire and are rewarded for decisiveness, efficiency, and action—not thoughtful reflection. That is why the right culture is so important.

The challenge is more than emotional; it's cognitive, too. Even without meaning to, we all favor evidence that supports our existing beliefs rather than alternative explanations. We also tend to downplay our responsibility and place undue blame on external or situational factors when we fail, only to do the reverse when assessing the failures of others—a psychological trap known as *fundamental attribution error.*

My research has shown that failure analysis is often limited and ineffective—even in complex organizations like hospitals, where human lives are at stake. Few hospitals systematically analyze medical errors or process flaws in order to capture failure's lessons. Recent research in North Carolina hospitals,

Designing Successful Failures

Perhaps unsurprisingly, pilot projects are usually designed to succeed rather than to produce intelligent failures—those that generate valuable information. To know if you've designed a genuinely useful pilot, consider whether your managers can answer yes to the following questions:

- Is the pilot being tested under typical circumstances (rather than optimal conditions)?

- Do the employees, customers, and resources represent the firm's real operating environment?

- Is the goal of the pilot to learn as much as possible (rather than to demonstrate the value of the proposed offering)?

- Is the goal of learning well understood by all employees and managers?

- Is it clear that compensation and performance reviews are not based on a successful outcome for the pilot?

- Were explicit changes made as a result of the pilot test?

published in November 2010 in the *New England Journal of Medicine*, found that despite a dozen years of heightened awareness that medical errors result in thousands of deaths each year, hospitals have not become safer.

Fortunately, there are shining exceptions to this pattern, which continue to provide hope that organizational learning is possible. At Intermountain Healthcare, a system of 23 hospitals that serves Utah and southeastern Idaho, physicians' deviations from medical protocols are routinely analyzed for opportunities to improve the protocols. Allowing deviations and sharing the data on whether they actually produce a better outcome encourages physicians to buy into this program. (See "Fixing Health Care on the Front Lines," by Richard M. J. Bohmer, HBR, April 2010.)

Motivating people to go beyond first-order reasons (procedures weren't followed) to understanding the second- and third-order reasons can be a major challenge. One way to do this is to use interdisciplinary teams with diverse skills and perspectives. Complex failures in particular are the result of multiple events that occurred in different departments or disciplines or at different levels of the organization. Understanding what happened and how to prevent it from happening again requires detailed, team-based discussion and analysis.

A team of leading physicists, engineers, aviation experts, naval leaders, and even astronauts devoted months to an analysis of the *Columbia* disaster. They conclusively established not only the first-order cause—a piece of foam had hit the shuttle's leading edge during launch—but also second-order causes: a rigid hierarchy and schedule-obsessed culture at NASA made it especially difficult for engineers to speak up about anything but the most rock-solid concerns.

Promoting Experimentation

The third critical activity for effective learning is strategically producing failures—in the right places, at the right times—through systematic experimentation. Researchers in basic science know that although the experiments they conduct will occasionally result in a spectacular success, a large percentage of them (70% or higher in some fields) will fail. How do these people get out of bed in the morning? First, they know that failure is not optional in their work; it's part of being at the leading edge of scientific discovery. Second, far more than most of us, they understand that every failure conveys valuable information, and they're eager to get it before the competition does.

In contrast, managers in charge of piloting a new product or service—a classic example of experimentation in business—typically do whatever they can to make sure that the pilot is perfect right out of the starting gate. Ironically, this hunger to succeed can later inhibit the success of the official launch. Too often, managers in charge of pilots design optimal conditions rather than representative ones. Thus the pilot doesn't produce knowledge about what *won't* work.

In the very early days of DSL, a major telecommunications company I'll call Telco did a full-scale launch of that high-speed technology to consumer households in a major urban market. It was an unmitigated customer-service disaster. The company missed 75% of its commitments and found itself confronted with a staggering 12,000 late orders. Customers were frustrated and upset, and service reps couldn't even begin to answer all their calls. Employee morale suffered. How could this happen to a leading company with high satisfaction ratings and a brand that had long stood for excellence?

A small and extremely successful suburban pilot had lulled Telco executives into a misguided confidence. The problem was that the pilot did not resemble real service conditions: It was staffed with unusually personable, expert service reps and took place in a community of educated, tech-savvy customers. But DSL was a brand-new technology and, unlike traditional telephony, had to interface with customers' highly variable home computers and technical skills. This added complexity and unpredictability to the service-delivery challenge in ways that Telco had not fully appreciated before the launch.

A more useful pilot at Telco would have tested the technology with limited support, unsophisticated customers, and old computers. It would have been designed to discover everything that could go wrong—instead of proving that under the best of conditions everything would go right. (See the sidebar "Designing Successful Failures.") Of course, the managers in charge would have to have understood that they were going to be rewarded not for success but, rather, for producing intelligent failures as quickly as possible.

In short, exceptional organizations are those that go beyond detecting and analyzing failures and try to generate intelligent ones for the express purpose of learning and innovating. It's not that managers in these organizations enjoy failure. But they recognize it as a necessary by-product of experimentation. They also realize that they don't have to do dramatic experiments with large budgets. Often a small pilot, a dry run of a new technique, or a simulation will suffice.

. . .

The courage to confront our own and others' imperfections is crucial to solving the apparent contradiction of wanting neither to discourage the reporting of problems nor to create an environment in which anything goes. This means that managers must ask employees to be brave and speak up—and must not respond by expressing anger or strong disapproval of what may at first appear to be incompetence. More often than we realize, complex systems are at work behind organizational failures, and their lessons and improvement opportunities are lost when conversation is stifled.

Savvy managers understand the risks of unbridled toughness. They know that their ability to find out about and help resolve problems depends on their ability to learn about them. But most managers I've encountered in my research, teaching, and consulting work are far more sensitive to a different risk—that an understanding response to failures will simply create a lax work environment in which mistakes multiply.

This common worry should be replaced by a new paradigm—one that recognizes the inevitability of failure in today's complex work organizations. Those that catch, correct, and learn from failure before others do will succeed. Those that wallow in the blame game will not.

Originally published in April 2011. Reprint R1104B

Discussion Guide

Are you feeling inspired by what you've read in this collection? Do you want to share the ideas in the articles or explore the insights you've gleaned with others? This discussion guide offers an opportunity to dig a little deeper, with questions to prompt personal reflection and to start conversations with your team.

You don't need to have read the book from beginning to end to use this guide. Choose the questions that apply to the articles you have read or that you feel might spark the liveliest discussion.

Reflect on key takeaways from your reading to help you adopt the ideas and techniques you want to integrate into your work as a leader. What tools can you share with your team to help everyone be their best? Becoming the leader you want to be starts with a detailed plan—and a commitment to carrying it out.

1. What are some examples of disruptive innovations and sustaining innovations in your industry? Can you think of entrants into your market that you may be overlooking as a threat because they are targeting lower-end or unprofitable customer segments? What opportunities do you see for your company to *be* the disrupter—entering underserved markets or creating simpler, cheaper solutions that could scale up?

2. What nondisruptive opportunities (innovations addressing accepted but unmet needs) can you imagine in your industry? As outlined in the chapter by Kim and Mauborgne, Square extended the reach of credit cards rather

than displacing them. Where could your company similarly augment existing products and services? How are your organization's resources and attention allocated between disruptive and nondisruptive innovations, and what's the right mix?

3. How are day-to-day operations overshadowing long-term innovation on your team? What legacy mindsets, practices, or conventions (even those that are well intended) are keeping you stuck in the past? What high-risk, high-opportunity projects could you start or accelerate to enhance "Box 3" efforts to invent tomorrow?

4. How is the idea of an "innovation basket," as described in "A New Approach to Strategic Innovation," different from the traditional innovation portfolio? What current metrics do you have in place to help assess the strategic fit of innovation initiatives, and how well have these mechanisms worked? Consider whether several current or past innovation initiatives fit well with your organization's strategy.

5. After reading "A Refresher on Discovery-Driven Planning," what surprises you about this classic framework? According to the article, DDP works best for exploratory ventures rather than predictable ones. What current projects would benefit from DDP principles or processes, and what past projects might have gone differently if DDP was used?

6. What "jobs" do your customers hire your products or services to perform, and how well are they performing those jobs? Which customer jobs are currently poorly executed or not being done in the marketplace? Can you think of examples (from your industry or another) of work-arounds

customers already use to get their jobs done—and what unmet needs these hacks might reveal?

7. What specific behaviors related to innovation do you want to encourage on your team, and what's blocking them (think of ingrained habits, rituals, and routines)? What interventions might help you overcome key creativity blockers? What "innoganda" (innovation propaganda that was all for show) efforts have failed in your organization in the past, and what can you do to ensure that interventions don't fall flat going forward?

8. Does your team have enough freedom to explore while also maintaining enough discipline to move ideas forward? How can you ensure that productive disagreements surface weaknesses that will help strengthen new ideas without fracturing the team? What changes might help people embrace constructive conflict more?

9. What cognitive biases—such as functional fixedness, design fixation, and goal fixedness—are prevalent in your organization, and how do they show up in problem-solving? What specific examples can you offer of times when these or other biases have hampered innovation? What changes would you recommend to produce better, more-novel ideas?

10. What are the primary lessons of reverse innovations (innovations created first for emerging markets before being exported to more-developed economies)? Why do you think there haven't been more successful examples? What opportunities for reverse innovations can you imagine in your industry?

11. Is AI likely to be most effective for process improvements, recombination of existing elements, or radical break-throughs in your team or organization? How might you integrate AI into existing processes to support creative recombination instead of just making incremental tweaks?

12. How often and effectively does your team engage with users through empathy and real-world observation to uncover latent needs? In what ways does design think-ing extend beyond solving customers' problems to help employees with the innovation process itself? How is your team or organization capitalizing on these internal applications—or not?

13. How can you cultivate the right skills and mindset to improve innovativeness on your team? How could you or your team leader be a more effective "chaos pilot" (as the authors of "If Your Innovation Effort Isn't Working, Look at Who's on the Team" call it)?

14. What are the main ways your offerings have improved over time (in terms of price, performance, etc.)? How might understanding these changes help you guess which improvements will matter in the future? (See "What's Your Best Innovation Bet?" for more ideas.) How can you pre-pare to pivot if the market or technology shifts or some-thing new and better than your offering comes along? How can you ensure that everyone in your organization or on your team understands your innovation goals and where to focus their attention?

15. What separates "intelligent failures" from other types of failure? What mechanisms are in place to ensure that

people in your organization or on your team feel it's safe to speak up about early signs of failure? How could you improve levels of psychological safety and ensure that the right kind of failure is valued and useful, not punished?

16. What other sources on innovation have had a significant impact on your work? Were there voices or subtopics you missed in this collection? Were there voices or subtopics included that surprised you?

17. After reading and reflecting on this book and discussing it with people on your team, write down the ideas and techniques you want to try. Think of how you might experiment and implement those in both the short term and long term. Draft a plan to move forward.

Notes

Quick Read: Great Innovators Create the Future, Manage the Present, and Selectively Forget the Past

1. Charles A. O'Reilly III and Michael L. Tushman, "Organizational Ambidexterity: Past, Present and Future," May 11, 2013, https://www.hbs.edu/faculty/Pages/item.aspx?num=45551.

Quick Read: Can AI Help Your Company Innovate? It Depends

1. Michael Park, Erin Leahey, and Russell J. Funk, "Papers and Patents Are Becoming Less Disruptive Over Time, *Nature* 613 (2023): 138–144, https://doi.org/10.1038/s41586-022-05543-x.

2. Derek Saul, "Ozempic Sales Up 58% as Drugmaker Novo Nordisk Nets Record Profits," *Forbes*, November 2, 2023, https://www.forbes.com/sites/dereksaul/2023/11/02/ozempic-sales-up-58-as-drugmaker-novo-nordisk-nets-record-profits/.

3. Nancy Lapid, "Lilly's Mounjaro Leads to More and Faster Weight Loss Than Novo Obesity Drug, Data Analysis Finds," Reuters, November 27, 2023, https://www.reuters.com/business/healthcare-pharmaceuticals/lillys-mounjaro-leads-more-faster-weight-loss-than-novo-obesity-drug-data-2023-11-27/.

4. Sam Ransbotham and Shervin Khodabandeh, "Prototypes, Pilots, and Polymers: Cooper Standard's Chris Couch," May 11, 2021, in *Me, Myself, and AI*, podcast, https://sloanreview.mit.edu/audio/prototypes-pilots-and-polymers-cooper-standards-chris-couch/.

5. "Tyres Uncovered: The Secrets of the Compounds Which Help Us Travel In Comfort," Pirelli, October 11, 2016, https://www.pirelli.com/global/en-ww/road/cars/tyres/tyres-uncovered-the-secrets-of-the-compounds-which-help-us-travel-in-comfort-50391/.

6. Carrie Arnold, "Inside the Nascent Industry of AI-Designed Drugs," *Nature Medicine* 29 (2023): 1292–1295, https://doi.org/10.1038/s41591-023-02361-0; Jeff Walsh, "Machine Learning: The Speed-of-Light Evolution of AI and Design," Autodesk, May 5, 2016, https://www.autodesk.com/design-make/articles/machine-learning.

7. Sam Ransbotham and Shervin Khodabandeh, "AI and the COVID-19 Vaccine: Moderna's Dave Johnson," July 13, 2021, in *Me, Myself, and AI*, podcast, https://sloanreview.mit.edu/audio/ai-and-the-covid-19-vaccine-modernas-dave-johnson/.

8. Ransbotham and Khodabandeh, "Prototypes, Pilots, and Polymers."

9. *Ma(n)chine Learning: Pirrelli Annual Report 2022*, https://corporate.pirelli.com/corporate/en-ww/investors/the-editorial-project-2022/ai-pirelli.

10. Lynn Wu , Lorin Hitt, and Bowen Lou, "Data Analytics, Innovation, and Firm Productivity," *Management Science* 66, no. 5 (October 15, 2019), https://doi.org/10.1287/mnsc.2018.3281; Lynn Wu, Bowen Lou, and Lorin Hitt, "Data Analytics Supports Decentralized Innovation," *Management Science* 65, no. 10 (July 24, 2019), https://doi.org/10.1287/mnsc.2019.3344.

11. Shana Potash, "Chinese Researchers Discovered Effectiveness of Artemisinin Against Malaria," *Global Health Matters* 14, issue 5 (September/October 2015), https://www.fic.nih.gov/News/GlobalHealthMatters/september-october-2015/Pages/china-artemisinin-discovery.aspx.

Chapter 9: What's Your Best Innovation Bet?

1. "Mr. Shadow: A Song Composed with Artificial Intelligence," posted September 19, 2016, by Sony CSL (Paris), YouTube, https://www.youtube.com/watch?v=lcGYEXJqun8; "Daddy's Car: A Song Composed with Artificial Intelligence—in the Style of the Beatles," posted September 19, 2016, by Sony CSL (Paris), YouTube, https://www.youtube.com/watch?v=LSHZ_b05W7o.

2. "The Puffing Devil, Trevithick Day 2013," posted on April 27, 2013, by Cornish Trad, YouTube, https://www.youtube.com/watch?v=-y4Xzphnz6I.

About the Contributors

Scott D. Anthony is a clinical professor at Dartmouth College's Tuck School of Business and the author of *Epic Disruptions: 11 Innovations That Shaped Our Modern World* (Harvard Business Review Press, 2025).

Greg Brandeau is a former CTO at Pixar and Disney and now works with startups. He is a coauthor of *Collective Genius: The Art and Practice of Leading Innovation* (Harvard Business Review Press, 2014).

Clayton M. Christensen was the Kim B. Clark Professor of Business Administration at Harvard Business School and a frequent contributor to *Harvard Business Review*.

Paul Cobban is the former chief data and transformation officer at DBS Bank, based in Edinburgh, Scotland, and a coauthor of *Eat, Sleep, Innovate* (Harvard Business Review Press, 2020).

Karen Dillon is a former editor of *Harvard Business Review* and coauthor of *The Microstress Effect* (Harvard Business Review Press, 2023). She is also a coauthor of three books with Clayton Christensen, including the *New York Times* bestseller *How Will You Measure Your Life?*

David S. Duncan is the author of *The Secret Lives of Customers*. He was formerly a senior partner at the growth strategy consulting firm Innosight.

Amy C. Edmondson is the Novartis Professor of Leadership and Management at Harvard Business School. Her latest book is *Right Kind of Wrong: The Science of Failing Well*.

Nathan Furr is a professor of strategy at INSEAD and coauthor of five bestselling books: *The Upside of Uncertainty*, *The Innovator's Method*, *Leading Transformation*, *Innovation Capital*, and *Nail It Then Scale It*.

Amy Gallo is a contributing editor at *Harvard Business Review*, a cohost of the *Women at Work* podcast, and the author of *Getting Along: How to Work with Anyone (Even Difficult People)* (Harvard Business Review Press, 2022) and the *HBR Guide to Dealing with Conflict* (Harvard Business Review Press, 2017). She writes and speaks about workplace dynamics.

Vijay Govindarajan is the Coxe Distinguished Professor at Dartmouth College's Tuck School of Business; a Dartmouth-wide chair (the highest distinction awarded to faculty); a faculty partner in the Silicon Valley incubator Mach49; and senior adviser at the strategy consulting firm Acropolis Advisors. He is a *New York Times* and *Wall Street Journal* bestselling author. His latest book is *Fusion Strategy: How Real-Time Data and AI Will Power the Industrial Future* (Harvard Business Review Press, 2024).

Taddy Hall is a senior partner at the brand consultancy Lippincott leading the Experience Innovation and Engineering practice. He is a coauthor of *Competing Against Luck: The Story of Innovation and Customer Choice.*

Linda A. Hill is the Wallace Brett Donham Professor of Business Administration and faculty chair of the Leadership Initiative at Harvard Business School, the author of *Becoming a Manager* (Harvard Business Review Press, 2019), and a coauthor of *Being the Boss* (Harvard Business Review Press, 2019) and *Collective Genius* (Harvard Business Review Press, 2014).

Stelios Kavadias is the Margaret Thatcher Professor of Enterprise Studies in Innovation and Growth at the University of Cambridge's Judge Business School and the director of its Entrepreneurship Centre.

W. Chan Kim is a professor of strategy and management at INSEAD and codirector of the INSEAD Blue Ocean Strategy Institute in Fontainebleau, France. He is a coauthor of *Blue Ocean Strategy: How to Create Uncontested Market Space and Make the Competition Irrelevant* (Harvard Business Review Press, 2015) and *Beyond Disruption: Innovate and Achieve Growth Without Displacing Industries, Companies, or Jobs* (Harvard Business Review Press, 2023).

Jeanne M. Liedtka is a professor emeritus of business administration at the University of Virginia's Darden School of Business.

Kent Lineback spent many years as a manager and an executive in business and government. He is a coauthor of *Collective Genius* (Harvard Business Review Press, 2014).

Christoph Loch is a professor of operations and technology management at IESE Business School in Barcelona, Spain, and is the former Dean of the University of Cambridge's Judge Business School. He is also the Editor-in-Chief of Management Science, a premier business research journal.

Renée Mauborgne is a professor of strategy and management at INSEAD and codirector of the INSEAD Blue Ocean Strategy Institute in Fontainebleau, France. She is a coauthor of *Blue Ocean Strategy: How to Create Uncontested Market Space and Make the Competition Irrelevant* (Harvard Business Review Press, 2015) and *Beyond Disruption: Innovate and Achieve Growth Without Displacing Industries, Companies, or Jobs* (Harvard Business Review Press, 2023).

Tony McCaffrey is the chief technology officer of Innovation Accelerator.

Rory McDonald is the John Tyler Professor of Business Administration in the Strategy, Ethics, and Entrepreneurship area at the University of Virginia Darden School of Business. He is the coauthor, with Christopher Bingham, of *Productive Tensions: How Every Leader Can Tackle Innovation's Toughest Trade-Offs*.

Rahul Nair is now an Associate Partner at Bain.

Kyle Nel is the CEO and cofounder of Uncommon Partners, a behavioral transformation consultancy; the former executive director of Lowe's Innovation Labs; and a coauthor of *Leading Transformation: How to Take Charge of Your Company's Future* (Harvard Business Review Press, 2018).

Natalie Painchaud is senior director at Innosight and coauthor of *Eat, Sleep, Innovate* (Harvard Business Review Press, 2020).

Jim Pearson is the CEO of Innovation Accelerator.

Thomas Zoëga Ramsøy is a highly cited neuroscientist and the author of three bestselling books, including *How to Make People Buy, Introduction to Neuromarketing and Consumer Neuroscience,* and *Leading Transformation* (HBR Press, 2018). He is also the founder and CEO of Neurons and the International Center for Applied Neuroscience.

Sam Ransbotham is a professor of business analytics at Boston College's Carroll School of Management. He cohosts the *Me, Myself, and AI* podcast.

Michael E. Raynor is a director at Deloitte Consulting and coauthor of *The Three Rules: How Exceptional Companies Think.*

Melissa A. Schilling is the John Herzog Professor of Management at New York University's Stern School of Business and author of *Quirky: The Remarkable Story of the Traits, Foibles, and Genius of Breakthrough Innovators Who Changed the World.*

Haijian Si is the former CEO of Chinese new energy companies Linuo Power Group Co., Huanyu Power, and Hanergy Thin Film Power and a doctoral candidate at the University of Cambridge's Judge Business School.

Emily Truelove is an assistant professor of business administration in the Organizational Behavior Unit at Harvard Business

School and a coauthor of *Collective Genius* (Harvard Business Review Press, 2014).

Amos Winter is the Robert N. Noyce Career Development Assistant Professor and director of the Global Engineering and Research Laboratory in the department of mechanical engineering at the Massachusetts Institute of Technology.

Lynn Wu is an associate professor at the Wharton School of the University of Pennsylvania. She teaches and researches the use and impact of emerging technologies on business.

Index